Table of Contents

Preface 2

Introduction 8

Overview 14
    Poem: The Flute Whisperer 15

Instrument Fluency and Artistry 28
    Poem: The Octave 29

Silence 40
    Poem: Liminal Space 41

Performance vs. Service 50
    Poem: The Shimmering 51

Know Your Listeners 58
    Poem: Soul Songs 59

Musical Modes Simplified 66

Rhythms 76
    Poem: Lyrical Dance 77

The Phenomenal Breath 88

Simple Melodic Phrases 96
    Poem: The Composition 97

Mileage and Commitment 110

Appendix of Extended Scale Intervals 116

Learn to Play for Ceremonies on the

NATIVE AMERICAN STYLE FLUTE

Create Your Musical Ministry

Ami Sarasvati, CMP

Copyright © 2026 Ami Sarasvati

All rights reserved

1st Edition

Paperback ISBN: 979-8-9883518-5-6

Transcribed in Nakai Flute Tablature courtesy of R. Carlos Nakai
Fingercharts courtesy of Clint Goss   www.NAFTracks.com
Logo artwork and Kokopellis created by Susan Englert: www.becreativesc.com
Cover design and book design by Lauren Kroll: www.laurenkroll.co
Special thanks to my amazing *Book Launch Team*

Get Your Free Gifts Now!

Receive valuable free resources to support your learning. Scan the QR code to visit:

www.learntoplayNAF.com

Note: The QR codes in this book take you to additional information, audio, or video files. You can access these links by opening the camera on your smart phone, holding it steady, and focus your camera on the QR code. **Touch the link on your phone screen to open.**

Preface

I can remember the moment I felt like I was finally in my element as a ceremonial flute player. I was attending a SoulCollage® retreat at **Spirit in the Desert Retreat Center in Carefree, AZ**. My group was in great hands with Kat Kirby, a long-time masterful facilitator and trainer, as our leader. Kat gave us directions, and a dozen ladies who seemed to know the routine went right to it. We were seated in small groups at tables all around the room. Sometimes, we created the cards in silence, and sometimes Kat played an awesome playlist for us softly.

On day one, I started wondering why I was at this retreat, what I was seeking in my life, and why we were making these fun and thought-provoking collage cards. In a sense, it was good to come to a SoulCollage® retreat with no idea of what it was. I was still not feeling aligned with my evolving potential, although I enjoyed teaching flute online and writing books. I hoped this retreat would give me a glimpse of what was uniquely *mine* to do.

Labyrinth at Ghost Ranch, Abiquiu NM

While taking a walk at lunchtime, I noticed there was a labyrinth on the retreat grounds. I thought back to the moment I first encountered a labyrinth. It was 2018, on a personal vision quest at **Ghost Ranch in Abiquiu, NM,** an hour north of Santa Fe. I had no idea what a labyrinth was then, and this time wasn't much different. I knew I was drawn to it, but I didn't know much about labyrinths.

Here again in my sight, at Spirit in the Desert, was a labyrinth. Again, I felt the invitation. I wondered if Kat had scheduled a labyrinth walk on our retreat. When I asked her about it, she said we were welcome to take a walk in the labyrinth, but there was nothing planned.

A spark ignited in me. I had a flute with me. I almost always bring a flute or two with me for playing opportunities! I could offer to play my flute for the group as they walked the labyrinth. The opportunity had indeed presented itself, tied in a big red bow. I asked Kat if that would be okay, and she said it would.

Kat let the group know that the next day, I would play for whoever wanted to walk the labyrinth after lunch. Some were interested, and some were so beautifully immersed in their SoulCollage® projects that they chose to stay in the room and continue on with their cards.

The next day after lunch, the moment had arrived to play for the group as they walked the labyrinth. I carefully paced my playing to support their time for contemplation as they walked. Completely improvised and fully present, I played very simply, with many generous silences between breaths. The peaceful feeling that came over me transported me to a space of deep reverence for life, the beautiful souls walking the labyrinth, and the gift of the moment. I felt like the flute was playing through me. Each breath was inspired by what was needed in the moment.

Labyrinth at Spirit in the Desert, Carefree AZ

In that space, I was a hollow bone, a hollow reed, a vessel for spirit to breathe through. I stayed in my heart, present to the walkers, letting my intuition guide me one breath at a time. It felt like time had slowed down and maybe even come to stillness. There we were, in a liminal space together, held by the labyrinth, supported by the flute music and its profound duet with silence.

One of the retreat participants, Connie, had become my fast friend. I felt *seen* by Connie. We talked about our struggles as women and mothers. We shared a soul connection as two women, walking our path. She knew I had been struggling with being homesick for my children and friends back in the Northeast.

After Connie finished her labyrinth walk, she came right over to me. She spoke softly and directly to my soul when she said, "That is why you're here." I knew she was talking about what just happened during her labyrinth walk, supported by my flute playing. I felt fully embodied, fully aligned, fully illuminated with something greater than myself that was still present. The ceremonial flute playing had opened up a channel inside me that was now fully activated. Since then, Connie's words have echoed in my heart many times and have become a guiding light for me. She gave me the glimpse I was looking for at this retreat. That moment was a turning point.

As life went on, I could see the magnitude of its influence on the trajectory of my musical and spiritual life.

Trained as a therapeutic musician, I already had significant experience playing for the ill and dying, which is another way of playing in service. Playing for a ceremony was a new direction for my musical and spiritual calling.

Since that retreat at *Spirit in the Desert*, I have been blessed with numerous opportunities to play for a variety of ceremonies, many in-person and some online. Accompanying labyrinth walks became a new, regular opportunity for this style of playing.

Flutes Have Been Played for Thousands of Years

The role of the ceremonial flute player may essentially be the same as it was thousands of years ago when played by medicine men and women, shamans, priests, and other ceremonial musicians. In this role, just like our flute-playing ancestors, we become an empty vessel for the song of the ceremony. The more we can allow this energy to move through us, the more the music will play itself.

In this sublime space, we are intuitively guided as we play, and the tones come through our flute. We may find ourselves playing while somehow walking in two worlds, always keeping a soft, steady gaze on what is happening, while providing a sonic atmosphere that helps people go deeper into themselves. In that interior space, we can listen to the whispers of the soul.

The time is now, dear reader, to sing the glorious song of the flutes in ceremony, played live and with great heart. Be prepared for opportunities, expected and unexpected. One only needs to glance at the many groups on social media to see the global existence of Native American style flute (NAF) enthusiasts and groups. This instrument continues to grow in leaps and bounds due to its wide appeal.

When we hear the sound of the flute, energized by the player's breath, a deep connection often happens. There is a feeling conveyed from the flute that makes its way right to our hearts. Our bodies have been listening to the sound of flutes for generations and know the sound.

Creating a Musical Ministry

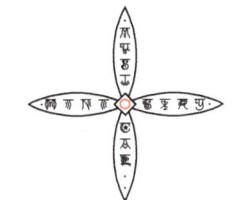

The words *musical ministry* came to me and seemed to fit the direction of my musical life. Ministry is a strong word with several connotations. Consider this definition of ministry: *the act of service or carrying out a specific function or role within a religious, spiritual, or humanitarian context.*

The notion of ministry, to me, is about the experience of feeling reverent as I play my flutes. It is a spacious, loving, connected, and supremely calm feeling. When I play for a ceremony, I feel I am at the intersection of my earthly abilities and divine purpose. That's how I define musical ministry for myself. Played skillfully and from the heart, the flute can transport people in a unique way. The flute has a hypnotic effect. It is wise to be aware of its abilities and powers.

If you have heard the calling of the flute in this way, then bring all your sensitivity, sincerity, and heart to this learning. May your learning be meaningful and useful. May every note you play be beautiful. May your playing be a source of service and healing.

 **Note: The QR codes in this book** take you to additional information, audio, or video files. You can access these links by opening the camera on your smart phone, holding it steady, and focus your camera on the QR code. **Touch the link on your phone screen to open.**

Scan the QR code to see an example of ceremonial flute playing for a labyrinth walk.

Playing for labyrinth walkers at Mercy Center in Burlingame CA

Introduction

First, a Word of Encouragement

If you desire to play simply and beautifully on your flute, you're in the right place. Don't be intimidated by anything in this book, from intervals to spiritual prose. You do not need to master everything covered in this book to start playing for ceremonies. These are recommendations based on experience, training, results, and feedback.

This style of playing is a path of artistry, simplicity, and silence. If you can play one note at a time beautifully on the flute, and can be in a constant duet with silence, you have found your on-ramp. With this approach in mind, let's explore how this style fits into various ceremonies and can even integrate with other practices.

Ceremonies Can Look a Thousand Ways

A word about *ceremonial style playing* and the scope of this book: ceremonial playing is a reverent style of playing an instrument that supports the intent of a ceremony or sacred moment.

Here are some examples from simple to grandiose:

- a personal prayer inside or outdoors
- a soul song to a friend
- a musical offering to the rising sun
- a harmonic thank you to a full moon
- a lyrical labyrinth walk by yourself or for a group
- welcoming a baby into the world
- supporting an artist retreat
- a contemplative interlude for people in grief
- a sweat lodge
- a Medicine Wheel walk
- a guided meditation
- and a thousand other variations where the music deepens the experience.

This style of playing is a path of artistry, simplicity, and silence.

Overall, this style of playing enhances a contemplative experience.

Bringing Ceremonial Style Playing to other Healing Arts Practices

Some ceremonial players may be yoga teachers who play for their students during the meditation at the end of the class. Massage therapists, acupuncturists, reflexologists, and other healing arts-oriented practitioners may find this style of playing to be a wonderful complement to their existing work.

Playing one-on-one for clients, as well as groups of any size, may be an appropriate setting to weave in ceremonial style music on the flute.

A Well-suited Instrument

The Native American style flute (NAF) has special attributes that make it uniquely wonderful and well-suited for this work. Certainly, any high-quality flute that has a calming voice would be suitable for this approach.

The approach presented in this book can be applied to other wind instruments, stringed instruments, the voice, and a variety of other instruments. There are considerations to be made depending on the instrument. Use common sense.

No Recognizable Melodies

This method intentionally discourages playing familiar melodies. Playing familiar songs creates expectations and shifts the focus from transformation to evaluation. When a listener hears a familiar melody, they drift to a space of evaluation of how well the melody is being played. If they know the melody, they cannot help notice if all the *correct* notes are being played.

In contrast, the improvisational style of playing presented in this book prepares the musician to play with sensitivity in the moment, in service to others, and provides a soundscape for transformation. Simple improvisation brings great freedom. Without the shackles of having to play a piece of music perfectly with its prescribed notes and tempo, a new world awaits you.

This style of playing draws the listener into a reverie. The approach is remarkably simple. You can start right away with the pentatonic minor scale. The pentatonic major scale is an important next step.

Over the long haul, a strong understanding of the chromatic intervals of the flute is a master key to skillful and artistic improvisation. This material is a secret garden welcoming you in when you are ready.

However, the sensitive and artistic use of the **pentatonic minor and major scales is enough** for a lifetime.

This style of playing draws the listener into a reverie.

Chapter Invitations

Each chapter will conclude with a **Chapter Invitation** to help you integrate the material in the chapter. There is no need to do these steps now. This is an overview of the process.

The Musical Mantras and Journaling Method

These invitations will help you process the information and give you clear insights on how to proceed. You can use the space provided in this book or get a special journal.

1. Go Inward with a Musical Breath Mantra

A musical breath mantra is used to move into a quiet interior space. Simple mantras are provided, or you can make up your own. Musical mantras are designed to be coordinated with the breath.

2. Listening, Witnessing, and Receiving

Once you've come to a more relaxed state and are focused inwardly, the veil between your everyday existence and the field of limitless possibilities is thin. Receive what comes to you with neutrality. Flashes, words, songs, and other inklings may come. Simply notice everything.

3. Journal on What Comes to You (writing prompts provided)

This is a private activity and is not intended for sharing. Really let it rip on the page, which is for your eyes only. Journaling in this way reveals your inner sparks and invites exploration. These prompts relate to the material in the chapter. They are catalysts for discovering and manifesting. You will be richly rewarded every time you accept these invitations.

4. Reviewing and Reflecting for Insights

Finally, you'll read what you just wrote, from a curious point of view. Your truths and dreams literally appear before your eyes on the page. Uncensored and completely private, you begin to get a perspective of your inner stirrings.

*Each **Chapter Invitation** is followed with a page like this so you can journal directly on this book or you can use a different journal.*

Overview

The Flute Whisperer

*She takes a breath
and blows a cloud
to the heavens
to the heavens*

*a harmony dances in mid air
moving and dispersing
then silence takes a turn
in this duet
in this duet*

*the flute whisperer
hidden but heard
blows another
blows another*

What is Ceremonial Playing?

Ceremonial playing is a reverent way of playing a musical instrument that enhances the atmosphere of a transformation. This style requires that the flute player come from a place of being in service and support to the ceremony's intention and the people attending. This is an overview of the major concepts of this playing style.

All ceremonies have a beginning, middle, and end.

- Sandra Ingerman, *Walking in Light*

Ceremony Anatomy

Intention

Playing flute in service requires a clear and beautiful intention for the ceremony. Providing appropriate, ceremonial music for an event takes the experience to a whole new level—a level where we float in the energy of the group, accessing the healing voice of the flute played with reverence. Your intention influences the overall experience and outcome of the ceremony and it is important that you are aware of that influence.

Tune in to the energy of the flute, the group, the place, and the intention of the ceremony. Many inspirations will likely flow, one breath at a time.

Playing a NAF in a ceremony begins with an inner invocation that is in alignment with the wisdom and grace of our highest musical self. Musicians have different rituals that help them step into a role of service. Some may begin by invoking ancestors, helpful compassionate helpers, the elementals and other spiritual forces. I start with three breaths which I explain later.

Our wise ancestors knew about the ways of the ground; they knew that the corn could not truly nourish, unless it was planted with prayer. It may grow physically, it may even be harvested, sold, and consumed, but it will not nurture the cells of the living, spirit-filled body, unless it is sown with reverence.

- From *The Ceremonial Circle* by Sedona Cahill & Joshua Halphern

Ceremonial Playing As It Relates To The Elements

There are many ways to play for ceremonies. Learning to use playing techniques to invoke the elements of earth, water, fire, air, and space is a worthy pursuit. In that system of playing, the flute would play other styles not covered in this book. This book focuses on a style of ceremonial playing that belongs to **air** and **space**, from an elemental point of view.

About the Elements

Briefly, any instrument, even a singing bowl, can be used to take people on a journey through all the elements, each invoking a certain energy. For example, in a sweat lodge, fire energy would be an important element to invoke at certain times.

As just mentioned above, but worth reinforcing, the focus of this book is how to play the flute in the elements of **air** and **space** primarily. Here is an overview to give you an idea of how to play to invoke the elements. These are broad descriptions and deserve independent study if you want to pursue this vast topic.

Earth Element Energy

Earth energy is invoked by playing a slow, rhythmic pulse. It provides stability, structure, and connection. It prepares us for water. When playing the flute, low tones work well here.

Water Element Energy

The Water Element is about playing with fluidity and adaptability. Melodic, pentatonic phrases work well. The water element is about emotion and movement. Play with flowing phrases and leave space for sensitivity. The water element represents liquidity.

Fire Element Energy

The Fire Element uses rhythms to invoke sparking energy. Envision a fire crackling and popping, rattles shaking, percussion voices alive, and dynamics evolving. The flutes are wonderful as they can be played as percussion instruments by using articulation techniques. Emotions are high in fire-element playing, and the rhythms are faster.

Air Element Energy

The Air Element *harmonizes* earth, water, and fire. A new form is revealed. The phenomenal breath and silence are two main ingredients in the Air Element playing. Harmonies float in mid air, silences lull us in our interior world. It is a place for listening and floating.

To invoke the Air Element, there is no steady rhythm other than simple short and long notes. We play rubato especially here.

Qualities invoked include stillness, openness, awareness, unification, and release. We create a container and then hold that space for others to experience this profound element.

Space Element Energy

The Space Element is the most powerful space in healing practice. Here we can extend the sense of time. It takes full advantage of the spacious silence in between. It invokes the space between worlds, between realities, between breaths. Here is the final stage in the work of transformation.

We play so that listeners can integrate, assimilate, step into a new form, embody a new state, ground it, and manifest their intention. It is a boundless realm that allows us to empty our perceived self into a larger experience.

Using the flute, we can certainly take people through an elemental journey. We would play in the various ways mentioned. However, the focus of this book is a subset of an entire elemental journey. Now you have a perspective of the pages ahead and how they fit into a full spectrum of elemental playing on the flute.

The Space In Between Two Worlds Where the Flute Takes Us: Liminal Space

What is *liminal space*? From the Latin *limen*, meaning "threshold." This mysterious space is hard to define but unmistakably experienced. It is between ordinary modes of awareness—our everyday earthly world and our imaginal world. Liminal space is often where transformation happens. Since ceremonies are created to transform, it is important that we discover for ourselves how to create this elusive experience with our flutes played in a ceremonial way. The transcendent timbre of the flute can help listeners withdrawal from analytical thinking and transport them into a receptive, expansive space.

The Evolution from Performing Musician to Ceremonial Musician

There are full chapters on *Performance vs. Service* and *Know Your Listeners* because both topics are essential philosophies underlying this work. Here it is in a condensed form.

Know Your Listeners

Consider why people are attending the ceremony. They have come together in community to have an experience. How you fit into that experience is a delicate matter. The bottom line is to ensure you are truly playing from your heart and enhancing the experience. Remember to be mindful of the power of the flute. Be a *flute whisperer* in a ceremony—inviting the whispers of the participants' souls. The flute player supports the moment in an appropriate, sensitive manner.

Appropriateness

The voice of the flute is very powerful. One only needs to observe what happens when someone starts playing a flute to know this. Something activates within the listeners, and they instinctively turn their ears to the sound of the flute. In this sense, we need to consider how much attention should be given to the flute music and regulate our playing so that it supports the event without taking over energetically and becoming the event itself.

Flute Selection

When selecting flutes for an event, consider the purpose of the ceremony and the environment in which you will play. Also, consider whether you will be playing indoors or outside. High-pitched flutes are not suitable for most indoor occasions. A NAF on the lower end of mid-range, such as an F#, E, or D, will be best indoors. A bass flute can work as well. When considering a drone flute (double-chamber flute), I generally reserve it for ceremonies where I will be playing for a longer period of time and want to add variety to the sound for a while.

Create a Personal Mantra

Consider developing a mantra; a few words that instantly take you to your reverent state. When we need to transition quickly from setting up instruments and microphones to playing for ceremony, a mantra can be a useful tool.

My Mantra

My mantra came to me this way: when learning to play a rim-blown flute, the flute of the ancients seemed to hide its secrets from me. After a long time trying, I finally relaxed inwardly, and continued to inhale, forming my mouth and lips into yet another possible variation that might miraculously yield a sound from this flute, and exhaled into the wooden tube. Standing out in nature, trying again and again, I got an inspired message as I inhaled, "the breath of God." I exhaled, and suddenly the instrument gifted me with my first deep, rich sound from a rim-blown flute. I'm not sure which was the greatest gift—the beautiful sound or the mantra, but I am grateful for this message. I use it as my personal mantra with every breath I take in ceremony.

You can use or substitute the word "God" with any word that speaks to you—Goddess, Holy Spirit, Great Spirit, the Universe, Mystery, Eternal Source, all that is—the choice is yours. Others may call upon star beings, galactic families, or ancestors. Medicine Wheel practitioners may call in the four directions. Invoke the divine the way it works best for you. Connect with something that is expansive, meaningful, and empowering to you.

Always Play Beautifully

Every time you pick up the flute, strive to play each note beautifully. Whether you're playing a single note by yourself or you are playing for 10,000 people, I recommend always playing as beautifully as you can. This practice and philosophy will serve you well so that you don't take your playing too casually. There is a universe in every note you play. The more you immerse yourself in the magic of the sound, the more beautifully you will play. Co-create beauty with each breath. Between the notes is the blissful silence.

Silence

Silence is an entire chapter in this book as it is the most important element of ceremony. As a ceremonial player, you can take your listeners on a journey inward. This is done through partnering with silence. Silence is where we digest what we just heard. In ceremony, the openness of the silence is more important than the notes.

Preparation Overview

Preparing to play for a ceremony is an important step in creating a deep soundscape.

Set Up Beautifully and Properly

Even when you think you may be in a hurry, take a moment to set up properly and make your space visually pleasing. You are at a ceremony and you are there to enhance the event. Setting up is a special ritual. If your set up is attractive and honoring of the occasion, you can deliver beautiful sounds without the stress and distraction of fumbling around with flutes, mics (if you are using amplification), water bottles, jackets, etc. Keep your space looking great. Consider bringing a scarf, a cloth, or something to put over your belongings. Having a sturdy portable flute holder is ideal.

Placement of Yourself and Your Belongings

You may have control of where you will be placed when you play. If you do, take a look at the whole scene, consider where is best for you to put your belongings and how it could influence the event. In addition to your heart-centered, ceremonial flute playing, you are creating a sacred space for your flutes.

Before you play, take a moment to center yourself. Take a few deep breaths, look around you, and make sure you are comfortable, prepared, and organized. Use a mantra, visualization, or other ritual to put you in a reverent state. Be aware of the power of the flute. Play beautifully, enhance the playing with plenty of silence, and stay responsive.

An Opening Ritual

It is good to have a simple yet powerful invocation or ritual to transition yourself and a group into a ceremonial space. As ceremonial musicians, once we start to play, we have metaphorically pushed off from the shore.

My Beginning Ritual

Before the first note is played, of course, I carefully check and tighten the flute's bird (totem, fetish, block, etc.) as well as the placement of the microphone when amplified. Next, I begin with this simple ritual: I hold my flute horizontally and breathe at close range directly into the sound hole three times. I take my time. I allow time for the sweet silence in between the breaths. This ritual helps set the pace for me as well as the listeners.

Allow the wonderful emptiness between your breaths to slow everything down. Feel your connection with gravity. Balance from left to right, right to left, above to below, and below to above. Sense the beating of your heart. Bring something you adore into your heart. Feel the love. Connect with your desire to play in service. It is time to breathe into the flute.

As these breaths mark the beginning of the ceremony, I tune in to my body, tune in to the beings I am playing for, and tune in to my ministry. Once complete, this mini-ritual signals the transition from the beginning to the middle part of the ceremony. You are welcome to adopt this ritual and make it yours. Or, develop one that feels right to you. Keep it simple. Open yourself up to divine inspiration on every breath. Leave a little more silence after the invocation is complete. If you want to call in any energy, now is the time if you haven't already. From there, it is one breath at a time, one note at a time.

The Middle Part of the Ceremony

What to play? This book advocates for improvisational playing. No sheet music or music stands. Improvising exclusively keeps people out of their analytical minds and supports their sensory experience. Here is one approach I use quite frequently.

I choose a scale depending on the theme of the ceremony. I breathe into the flute three times. Next, I play the tonal center home note three times.

Next, I pick two more notes from the scale and initiate a dance between them, using short-LONG. No time signature. Just short-LONG. Keeping it extremely simple, I make great use of generous silences between every simple phrase I play. A complete description of this middle part of the ceremony and what to play is found in a dedicated chapter. But as a guideline, I use very simple melodic phrases and rhythmic patterns. Breath techniques, transitions, pacing, and generous uses of silence are just as important as the notes played.

Observe What is Happening

Most of my attention is on the people and the event. I time my playing thoughtfully with the energy and flow of the event. Remember to keep a soft, steady gaze on everything that is happening. Let each breath bring you fully into the present moment. Stay subtle and humble, listening to the whispers of intuition. One breath at a time. The *Rhythm* and *Simple Melodic Phrases* chapters provide choices for musically developing the middle part of the ceremony.

Bring the Ceremonial Playing to a Graceful and Harmonious Conclusion

When it is time to stop, come to a graceful conclusion. I keep a close watch on the timing of the ceremony. For example, if I'm playing for people walking a labyrinth, I watch for the very last person to exit the labyrinth, and continue to play for a short time, then gradually bring my playing to a gentle conclusion, landing on the home note. I may choose to play the home note up to three times, making each note a little longer than the one before it, which brings the soundscape back home and reinforces a conclusive feeling with each repetition.

My Ending Ritual

Just as I began, I conclude by holding the flute horizontally and breathing into the sound hole three times, taking my time and allowing for the sweet silence between breaths without rushing. This marks the end of the playing.

Be a Flute Whisperer

No sudden moves. Stay slow, stay present, even though the playing is over. Distracting movements or fiddling around with flutes, microphones, etc., will take away from the beautiful atmosphere that lingers in the air after the ceremonial playing is over. Be a *Flute Whisperer* and stay quiet. If possible, wait until the participants depart before you disassemble your setup.

Summary

As a society in the West, we hardly know ceremony and ritual unless it is part of a religious event, a birth or death, or a wedding perhaps. Yet, many of us hunger for ritual and ceremony in our everyday lives. It is only over the past few decades that healing arts venues such as yoga studios, community acupuncture clinics, sound healing events, and other forms of healing arts, have been emerging in many towns. These places offer a spiritual oasis in the community. Practitioners are adding and blending modalities to provide their people with a deeper sense of peace.

Playing the NAF for ceremonies is gorgeous work. It is a gift from the heavens to be of service in this way, especially with this enchanting instrument uniquely suited for spiritual work due to its connection to the breath.

One of the many gifts the NAF brings is the ease with which players can bring peace and light to our world. May that player be you, dear reader. May these pages guide you thoroughly and gently as you progress through the steps of becoming a ceremonial flute player for just the right occasions and opportunities.

In the chapters ahead, we will walk through each topic thoroughly.

The flute whisperer

hidden but heard

blows another

blows another

Chapter Invitation

1) Musical Breath Mantra

Come to a comfortable position. Bring your focus to your breath. Without changing anything or judging anything, just notice the rise and fall of your breath. [pause] Continue to quiet yourself by slowing and deepening your breath. Sink into a quiet space within. Feel your breath moving through your body. Tune in to the beating of your heart. Begin inhaling slowly and exhaling even more slowly. Let the words ride on your breath, going in and out.

Slowly *inhale*, "**Playing for**"

And *exhale* even slower, "**ceremonies**."

Go a little deeper into the stillness by repeating this mantra as your breath rides on the words as you inhale "**Playing for**" and exhale "**ceremonies**."

2) Meditate in this quiet space for a few minutes [pause]

3) Journaling Prompt

Gently deepen your breath and come back fully to the present space and time.
Take one minute to journal on this prompt:

As I breathed the words, **Playing for ceremonies***, one image that came to me is…*

4) Read what you just wrote

Circle or underline any words or phrases that jump out at you as you read. Maintain a compassionate, curious, and above all, non-judgmental attitude as you read. Look for clues and guideposts. Finally, journal once more reflecting on the words or phrases that jump out at you. Are there any surprises in your journaling?

Instrument Fluency and Artistry

The Octave

*Majestic at first sight
full of form and symmetry*

*reflecting diamonds
and inviting inquiry
evolved over time*

*balanced and perfect
majors and minors*

*mysteries and structures
shades and shapes*

*beckoning to be played
beckoning to be played*

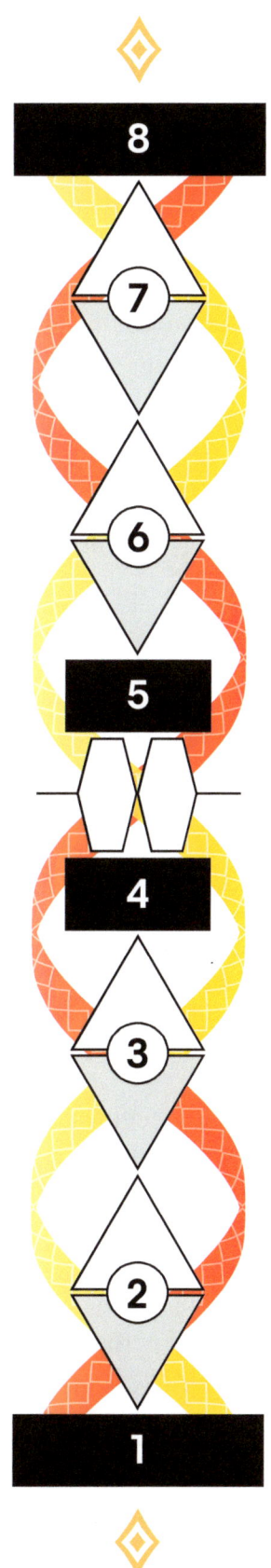

Are You Fluent on your Native American Style Flute?

Does your NAF feel like an extension of you when you play? If you are still trying to cover holes and understand the ideal breath volume on different regions of the flute, you have not yet achieved fluency, and your priority is to achieve foundational skills so you can focus on artistry.

There is a vast range in quality when it comes to flutes. Having a high-quality instrument is important, but don't rely on a fabulous flute to make fabulous music. Having the perfect flute that will play beautifully by virtue of something other than your ability is a bit of a fantasy. Your fluency and artistry are the most important ingredients—not the perfect flute, if there is such a thing. Every flute has its own secrets and personality, and it is in the skilled hands of the player that makes the flute sing beautifully. Your skill level, sensitivity, sense of adventure, and knowledge of the musical playing field will bring it all together.

Essential Music Theory

One of the fundamental teachings of musical expression is already contained in a beautiful structure we call the **octave**. Bring to mind the **Do-Re-Me** scale, the major scale. Between the bottom **Do** and one octave up to the next **Do** is our playing field. The notes within one **octave** can be sorted, combined, jumbled, and chosen in many ways. There are two built-in **pentatonic** scales that give us direct access to gorgeous music-making and that's all we need. Additionally, we can access different scales (modes) which is covered in a simplified way in this book and extensively in my book, *Discover the Musical Modes on the Native American Style Flute*.

The important concept is that these numbers have an emotional effect on listeners. When improvising, understanding intervals will give you the ability to shape tonal color, develop musical expression, and tell a musical story that supports ceremonies.

The playing field is 1 to 8. Each interval (see the numbers) has an explanation next to it. The number assigned is the distance from the **1**, the **1st interval**, the **tonal center**. So a 5 is only a 5 because it is 5 steps from the 1. The 1, the tonal center, is easily heard as it resolves music phrases and the overall song at the end. The rest of the notes have a job to do which evokes emotions. Use a keyboard or your voice, if possible. This framework is intended to simplify and clarify choices for you so that you can appreciate *why* you play which note, and *when*.

An Important Concept: Interval Function

A good piece of music is like a good story. Just as words form a story, your choice of notes creates meaning. Interval choices influence mood, direction, and musical expression. They all create varying *feelings* of tension and release, just like when you listen to a story.

In a *tiny* nutshell, each note of a mode or scale has a musical function. When playing music, first figure out what your **home** or **root** note is. That note is your **tonal center**. Even if a musical story (a song or improvisation) does not start on the root note, which is fairly common, it is important to look at the **last note of the song** to find out how it *resolves*. Then you'll know your **root note**. The ear senses the home note in a song or improvisation and then **seeks to return home** for resolution. Learn by playing and listening as you get to know the modes. Experiment *slowly* with the intervals and deeply listen for a sense of tension and release as you explore.

Here is a **snapshot** of **interval function** in relation to musical storytelling. You are encouraged to learn much more about intervals and their functions on your own.

1st Interval: Root (home/tonal center) - provides a sense of **stability** and **completeness**.

2nd Interval: Departure - you've left "home" but are still so close, creating a **pull back to home**.

3rd Interval: Mood/emotion - the defining interval of **major** (**bright** sound) or **minor** (**dark** sound).

4th Interval: Longing - the perfect 4th. Where does this interval **lead** you?

5th Interval: Harmonizing - the perfect 5th provides a highly **harmonious** sound.

6th Interval: Adds color - provides a distinctively **new color** and **sonic sensation**.

7th Interval: Anticipating and leading - gives the feeling of **almost** resolving.

8th Interval: Peak - a high point, an octave away from the root note. **Exhilarating** and satisfying!

Scan the QR code to watch a short video about **Interval Function**

The Notes

Fluency with at least the minor and major pentatonic scales is enough to work with to play for ceremonies. The two scales invoke two contrasting moods—the mysterious sound of the minor scale (Aeolian mode), and the uplifting sound of the major scale (Ionian mode). This is done very easily on the NAF.

You do not need extensive knowledge of musical modes to create a rich sound palette for ceremonial flute playing. You need the pentatonic minor and major scales, and an intention to play in service.

Fluency with the Notes

NAF players with any real mileage are aware of how sensitive the bottom hole can be, at least on some flutes. Make best friends with this note, for there is a whole universe in that note accessed through your breath. It lends itself to dynamics that are unique and expansive, like no other note on the instrument.

A thorough understanding of the chromatic scale (half-steps) within one octave is recommended but not required. See the Appendix in the back for chromatic scale and intervals in various starting positions on the instrument.

Getting Comfortable with Improvisation

An orchestral-level musician has achieved technical mastery, but when asked to play from the heart, and to play only by improvising, is that an area of mastery for them as well? Heartfelt musical artistry is a facet of fluency that requires basic technical mastery.

Soft Voice, Loud Voice

NAFs can vary widely in tonal quality and volume range. Some flutes with soft voices are perfect for quiet or small spaces, like in a hospice house or a massage room. Other flutes are better suited for large venues if they have a loud voice. Louder is not necessarily better. It is advisable to know your flutes and be strategic when it is time to play. Consider the space where you will play. You want to be able to play at an appropriate volume for the venue. If you plan to use amplification, it will also impact your choice of flutes.

Growing a Flute Forest

I have acquired and passed along many flutes. I keep approximately 30 flutes in my flute forest. The flute keys I pack up and use when playing for a ceremony are usually two Es, two or three Ds (which includes a drone), a C (EZ Anasazi flute which has a different tuning), and an F#.

Recommended Flute Keys for Ceremonies

It depends on the ceremony and the setting, but as a general guideline, I don't play anything higher than an F#. In order of priority of suggested flute keys, again my **recommendation** is:

A **E** (or two), a **D** (or two), a **C**, and maybe an **F#**. A drone flute of at least one of those keys can be a nice variation to the sound as well.

Consider having more than one flute of the same key if you play a lot in that key. Since the flutes wet out, you can only expect 15 to 30 minutes of quality playing time. Wetting out on an NAF refers to the phenomenon where moisture from the player's breath clogs up the flute's slow air chamber which blocks the airflow and causes the flute to stop playing. This is a normal occurrence due to the flute's design and can be influenced by the type of wood, the temperature of the air in which the flute is played, and the amount of moisture (saliva) the flute player puts into the flute when playing.

Choosing a Flute

Another area of instrument fluency is knowing how to choose a flute. When considering purchasing a NAF, try playing the flute yourself, if possible. If that is not feasible, consider obtaining a sound sample of it, if one is available. In addition to the sound of the NAF, keep in mind, especially if you have small hands, that the required reach of the holes is an important consideration. If you can't reach the holes and cover them properly, even though you love the sound of the instrument, then the flute will be unusable to you. We need to be comfortable with our instruments so that we are not challenged by dexterity. Of course, you want to be confident when you are playing your flute at ceremonies, so your flutes need to fit you ergonomically.

Flute Stands

It is fine to use a small blanket or towel to set your flutes down, but it is ideal to have a sturdy holder so they do not roll around and get knocked over. Good flute stands can be found online.

Protect Your Flutes

Protect your flutes by placing them in nicely padded individual flute bags when you transport them. Tube socks, one going over the bird and a second sock covering the bottom end of the flute, will work fine if you don't have nicely padded flute bags. Take care to protect your flutes from the weather. It may be okay if they are exposed for an hour or so when you play, but keep this in mind if you are playing outside regularly or for an extended time.

Other people may want to try out your flutes. I am protective of my flutes and do not allow others to handle or play them.

Amplification

Amplification is delightful and enhances your sound when set up correctly. I amplify with reverb whenever it is appropriate. However, keep in mind that flutes have been played for thousands of years without any amplification.

You can choose to amplify or not. I use a couple amplification systems. One is a battery-operated unit that I can carry around my shoulder like a purse. In most cases, this one is ideal. For large spaces, I use a Roland Street Boss amp with a Myers FeatherMic. The main desired effect is reverb. Even a karaoke machine with reverb, along with a lavaliere mic attached to the flute, can work.

An internet search will yield many options, but reverb is your best friend and a non-negotiable feature if you choose to amplify.

Assess Your Fluency

Assess your skill level on your NAF by taking this personal inventory. It is perfectly fine if you can't claim fluency on all these elements. Use them as a list to develop over time.

Finger Techniques

Fluently with the pentatonic minor scale
Ascending, descending, and jumping around the instrument with precision
Pitch bending (also listed in Breath Techniques below)
Grace Notes
Mordents and Inverted Mordents
Trills
Cross-fingering accurately, without undesirable transition sounds
Turns and Inverted Turns
Chirps
Finger Taps
Bending/Sliding
Runs /Glissando
Pop/Bark/Chirp

Breath Techniques

Tonguing vs. Slurring
Double and Triple Tonguing
Arcing notes
Volume control
Vibrato (slow, medium, and fast)
Pitch bending (also listed in Fingering Techniques)
Flutter-Tongue
Vocal Accents
and the most important breath technique of all... Generous Silences

Embracing Artistry

Now that we have a sense of what fluency is about, how does that interface with artistry? The enchanting quality of the flute is what touches our hearts and the hearts of listeners. Knowing the melodic effect you are creating will give you access to a world of musical storytelling. As you play, ask yourself, "What feeling does my music convey?"

Playing For Your Tribe

One student, Jack, was a tentative player. Jack had been taking lessons for well over a year and was still struggling with achieving technical prowess, yet when he put himself in an imaginary space of being in service, his regular tension seemed to vanish. At one lesson, I encouraged him to create a scene in his imagination where he would love to play in the ceremonial way. He came up with a beautiful visualization. In his imagination, he transported himself to a Reiki Retreat, where he played for his fellow Reiki Practitioners. His eyes drifted up, and he really went there in his heart. His playing instantly jumped a quantum leap. His artistry got tapped into by his desire to play for the *ceremony* and the *people*.

His desire to play for his fellow Reiki Practitioners caused him to tap into his heartfelt desire to be of service. From that place, his musical expression immediately eclipsed his previous level of playing. In a moment, he integrated all he had been working on and went to a place far higher than he had been able to access when trying to be technically proficient. What a difference it made in Jack's sound when he connected with his desire to play in service to his tribe.

Another student, Benny, was a quick learner. He picked up concepts and could run with them right away. Working with certain aspects of the flute, including fluency in the chromatic scale, Benny had an excellent command of articulation and fingering techniques. Benny, a Yoga Instructor, had started to play for sound baths and was loving it. He was getting great feedback by his participants. The environment made him rise to new levels at every event. His experience caused him to up-level his artistry by the mileage he was getting.

Both Jack and Benny are examples of how we can transition from being technicians to musicians playing in service to their beloved tribe.

What story would you like to tell on your flute?

Chapter Invitation

1) Musical Breath Mantra

Come to a comfortable position. Bring your focus to your breath. Without changing anything or judging anything, just notice the rise and fall of your breath. [pause] Continue to quiet yourself by slowing and deepening your breath. Sink into a quiet space within. Feel your breath moving through your body. Tune in to the beating of your heart. Begin inhaling slowly and exhaling even more slowly. Let the words ride on your breath, going in and out.

Slowly *inhale*, "**musical**"

And *exhale* even slower, "**fluency**."

Go a little deeper into the stillness by repeating this mantra as your breath rides on the words as you inhale "**musical**" and exhale "**fluency**."

2) Meditate in this quiet space for a few minutes [pause]

3) Journaling Prompt

Gently deepen your breath and come back fully to the present space and time.
Take one minute to journal on this prompt:

*As I breathed the words, **musical fluency**, I...*

4) Read what you just wrote

Circle or underline any words or phrases that jump out at you as you read. Maintain a compassionate, curious, and above all, non-judgmental attitude as you read. Look for clues and guideposts. Finally, journal once more reflecting on the words or phrases that jump out at you. Are there any surprises in your journaling?

Silence

Liminal Space

*May I stay here forever
in this liminal space
between the finite and the infinite
momentum released*

*listening to my soul song
as the notes pour out into the air
a melody forms and then vanishes
a long pause gives way to silence*

*a harmonic companion responds
another sublime silence
balances the dance between
above and below*

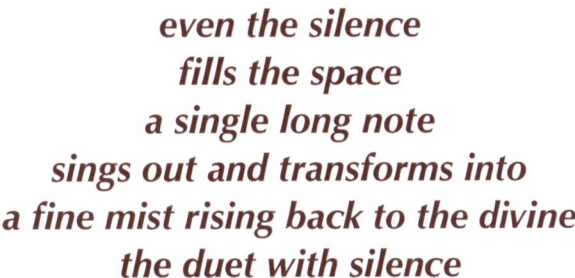

*even the silence
fills the space
a single long note
sings out and transforms into
a fine mist rising back to the divine
the duet with silence*

*in this liminal space
I am a vessel
for the eternal muse to whirl
in the space between
in the space between*

Silence

How comfortable are you with silence? In a world filled with devices, crowds, and busyness, how often do you experience silence? Imagine getting really comfortable with silence. There is a whole new gear to access using this method.

We are always in a duet with silence.

—Music for People

We slow everything down when we play in a duet with silence. One of your most important skills to master in ceremonial playing is to be artistic with silence. Consider the physiological, energetic, spiritual, and psychological value of what happens during silence, as widely documented and generally understood. This chapter aims to acknowledge and explore the application of silence in ceremonial playing. This material highlights the profound value of silence between the tones and how to dance with it.

The silence between musical phrases is where the listener goes deep. People breathe more deeply during generous silences, including the player. Take your time finding an easy pace in your dance with silence. Your ceremonial playing will reach a whole new level as you become fluent in the artistic use of silence. Silence and sound dance beautifully together.

A Paradigm Shift

What if the whole purpose of music was to create sublime moments of silence between the notes? In this style of playing, each and every musical phrase is balanced with an unhurried and often generous moment of silence. Then the next notes are played with the intention of setting up another experience of silence, then another.

Consider the experience that silence creates.

Silence invokes stillness.

Silence is the vacation, Shabbat, the winter, a time for rest and quiet.

Silence is where we catch glimpses of our light and infinite nature.

Silence is a precious and often unexpected gift.

Silence is where we exhale a little deeper.

Music is the silence

between the notes.

—Attributed to Debussy, Mozart, and others.

The Benefits of Silence

The Epoch Times ran an article in 2025 as Part 15 in a series called "Virtue Medicine." In 2006, Dr. Luciano Bernardi, Professor of Internal Medicine at Italy's University of Pavia and an enthusiastic amateur musician, designed an experiment to study the effects of music on the cardiovascular and respiratory systems of his participants.

Prof. Bernardi's paper, "A Quiet Medicine: How Silence Slows Down Your Heart and Grows Neurons" can be read in its entirety here:

https://pmc.ncbi.nlm.nih.gov/articles/PMC1860846/

From the article:

Bernardi randomly ordered six types of music and inserted two-minute "pauses" of silence to bring the subjects back to baseline—a control point for experiments. Yet contrary to his expectations, when the subjects listened to these pauses, they didn't return to baseline at all—instead, they relaxed.

In fact, they relaxed so much more profoundly during the silent pauses than during even the slowest, most soothing pieces of music that Bernardi had to rethink the whole premise of his experiment.

More:

In contrast, the two-minute rest randomly introduced into the sequence of tracks was characterized by the lowest systolic and diastolic blood pressure, [and] heart rate ... Interestingly, it was precisely during this short intermission, rather than during music, that we observed the greatest evidence of relaxation, as compared with baseline or music tracks.

###

Balancing the Sonic Environment

Another reason to use ample silence is to help balance the sonic environment. The power of the sound of a flute is evident. Let silence balance out the flute playing.

How long do we hold the silence?

This will vary as you develop your sensitivity to silence and timing, but for now, use your own unhurried breath cycle as the space for silence to take its turn.

Let's review. After you play a simple one-breath phrase, take a relaxed inhale and exhale cycle without playing. Then, on your next inhale, play your next musical phrase. Repeat and keep it intuitive.

Work toward getting really good at being in a duet with silence. To develop this ability, focus mostly on silence with this new awareness. Keep your choice of notes **repetitive** and **basic**.

After you play a simple one-breath phrase, take a relaxed inhale and exhale cycle without playing.

Then, on your next inhale, play your next musical phrase. Repeat and keep it intuitive.

Dwell in simplicity.

Inhale and exhale, letting silence take its turn, then it is your turn again. What is happening there? Listen to what silence whispers. Silence is the space of mystery, divine inspiration, and musical alchemy.

We Sometimes Audiate During Silence

What does it mean to audiate? We do it all the time. Here's what it is.

"Happy birthday to you…"

When you play the song in your head, you recall the tune from memory. We do it all the time.

A Story of Audiating: Your Listeners Remember

During the Veriditas Labyrinth Summer School in 2025, at the beautiful Mercy Center in Burlingame, California, I had the great honor of playing for the group multiple times. I played during labyrinth walks, meditations, the graduation for those who participated in the facilitator training, and other moments.

Halfway through the week, we had a little free time in the schedule one afternoon. Three of us took a taxi into San Francisco to Grace Cathedral to walk the magnificent labyrinth. When we arrived at Grace Cathedral, we were informed that it was closed for deep cleaning. Grace Cathedral has an indoor labyrinth, which we planned to walk, as well as an outdoor labyrinth.

Instead of being upset, the three of us turned our attention to the outdoor labyrinth just outside the doors of Grace Cathedral.

I did not bring a flute with me that day. We walked the labyrinth in silence. We were in no rush. The city was alive with people and trolleys. I, for one, was able to tune out the external noises and enjoy the walk. It was a gorgeous day in downtown San Francisco, and being there with my two new soul sisters was so meaningful.

On the ride home, we discussed our experience of the outdoor labyrinth walk. The other two women surprised me, and probably each other. They both reported that they heard me playing my flute during the walk. Again, I hadn't brought a flute with me that day. One of the ladies told me that she actually looked over at me to see if I was playing, but then saw I wasn't. Yet she was still audiating the flute music I had played during her walks at Summer School over the past few days.

The listeners entrain to your pace and sound. They may carry that memory, even without your presence, with them always.

Fascinating! This astounded me, and I think it's a great example of how we create a sound memory for the listeners when we play. It is good to be fully aware of this. A deep connection is made and remembered in the body.

Audiating is something we all do. It is important to recognize the power of music. The listeners entrain to your pace and sound. They may carry that memory, even without your presence, with them always.

In summary, simple phrases followed by generous silences work best.

Chapter Invitation

1) Musical Breath Mantra

Come to a comfortable position. Bring your focus to your breath. Without changing anything or judging anything, just notice the rise and fall of your breath. [pause] Continue to quiet yourself by slowing and deepening your breath. Sink into a quiet space within. Feel your breath moving through your body. Tune in to the beating of your heart. Begin inhaling slowly and exhaling even more slowly. Let the words ride on your breath, going in and out.

Slowly **inhale**, "**I listen**"

And **exhale** even slower, "**to the silence.**"

Go a little deeper into the stillness by repeating this mantra as your breath rides on the words as you inhale "**I listen**" and exhale "**to the silence.**"

2) Meditate in this quiet space for a few minutes [pause]

3) Journaling Prompt

Gently deepen your breath and come back fully to the present space and time.
Take one minute to journal on this prompt:

As I breathed the words, ***I listen to the silence****, I...*

4) Read what you just wrote

Circle or underline any words or phrases that jump out at you as you read. Maintain a compassionate, curious, and above all, non-judgmental attitude as you read. Look for clues and guideposts. Finally, journal once more reflecting on the words or phrases that jump out at you. Are there any surprises in your journaling?

Performance vs. Service

The Shimmering

*I want to go higher
higher and higher
back among the stars
with my brothers and sisters
where I belong*

*I want to travel lighter
lighter and lighter
no longer burdened
with doubt and hurt
so I can float
like the dry and ready seed head
of a dandelion ready and waiting
to take flight
inspired by a wish*

*I want to go deeper
deeper and deeper
into the depths of my heart
where the true light rests
in communion*

*I want to be free
more and more free
the rush of life behind me
no longer my story*

*I want to be quiet
so very still and quiet
where I can listen and hear
the shimmering above me
the beautiful shimmering
alive and illuminated*

An Ancient Practice

Ceremonial playing is an ancient, historically rich practice. All over the world, in every culture, ceremonial musicians have played for the people attending transformational events. The power of music, played with great heart and artistry, can take a ceremony to a whole new level.

Your Role

As a ceremonial player, your role is different than being a performer. You are there to be in service to the ceremony and support the people attending. If you're used to performing, it's important to internally adjust your approach. This role is entirely different than what you have done in the past, or would do in a performance.

You are at the ceremony to enhance the atmosphere of the event, in service to the attendees. Ceremonies are events in which a transformation is sought. The transformation is the focal point, even if it is as simple as a poetry reading among friends. The musical support is just that—support. Remember that people are there for the ceremony, not primarily the music.

Live Music vs. Recordings

When live music is played at a ceremony, it is a far cry from a CD playing on a machine. Even though there is much sublime recorded music available for Native American style flute, there is something entirely different about the experience of live music.

There are nearly limitless inspirations found in recordings from R. Carlos Nakai, Gary Stroutsos, Bryan Akipa, Coyote Oldman, Michael DeMaria, and dozens, if not hundreds, of other talented recording artists on the Native American style flute. However, a recording cannot turn down its own volume as a sudden cry of a bird is heard overhead. A recording cannot pull back in reverence to the sound of a strong wind that suddenly came up.

The unfolding of a ceremony also dictates what is played, how it is played, and when it is played. Expect the unexpected and be ready to respond in the moment. Unplanned events happen frequently in ceremonies, and the more you are present to the moment, the more the live, ceremonial flute music can be in harmony if a surprise event occurs.

The Art of Playing in Service

The art of playing in service requires staying entirely present. Your presence as a witnessing, influencing, and highly responsive compassionate musician holds a special role in the ceremony. You are walking in two worlds to co-create a sacred atmosphere that transports the listeners to a deeper space where they can breathe, especially during the generous silences you provide.

Invite the breath of the universe to play through you. Become a hollow reed. After silence takes its turn in the duet you are in with the sacred void, you invite the next breath to play through you again. You are an open vessel. Yes, you have half a plan, but the ceremony itself, with your keen intuition, guides the playing as you observe and support the ceremony.

Remember to pay attention to what is happening so you can pivot on a dime at any moment. As previously mentioned, playing familiar melodies is restrictive. In contrast, improvising while playing beautifully, you can be responsive and flexible.

The music creates a melodic and hypnotic atmosphere. You are tuned in, intuiting what sounds support this ceremony moment by moment. After each breath, provide a generous silence.

One way you may know you have made this profound internal shift from performing to playing in service is that your anxiety level may disappear. Not being the central focal point will banish your nervousness.

Pam's Story

Pam discovered the flute in her 60s. She took to the flute right away and learned to play the instrument quickly. She played with friends, performed for her church, collaborated with other musicians, and even attended a large flute school, where she held her own among the best players.

In her 70s, at Christmas time, she offered to play at her church. She chose a traditional Christmas song that she knew by heart. She considered it a simple piece she would have no problems playing. When it came time for her solo, all eyes and ears were on her. She started the song everyone knew so well. Then disaster struck. For some unknown reason, during her solo, in her words, her "fingers just wouldn't go where they were supposed to go. It was horrible! It was an awful feeling." The event was devastating to her, and she swore she would never play in public again.

Two years later, she decided she would learn to play in this ceremonial way. Something opened up inside her. With no familiar and predictable melody to memorize and perform, she gently began to explore this style and started to enjoy playing her beloved flutes again.

Around the same time as she was learning this style, one of the members of her church fell ill. After battling for her life for over a year, Pam's friend passed away. It was shocking to the community as the woman was fairly young, and it was deeply sad for Pam. Aside from the formal service commemorating her friend's passing, Pam thought it would be healing to have a grief circle for those in the congregation affected by the woman's passing.

In honor of the occasion, Pam decided she would offer simple flute music to support the grief circle. Recognizing the weight of the event, she took extra care to prepare herself by choosing an outfit that was ceremonial but not showy. She did not want to draw attention to herself. Before the grief circle ceremony, Pam set up her space ahead of time, complete with a small blanket where her flute rested until it was time to play. Pam recalls, "It made my surroundings feel sacred, a place just for me. It was very important to me."

As the 30 men and women began to gather, Pam played while they seated themselves in a circle. She intentionally chose her place outside the circle. "They were in a circle and I was outside the circle, not at the head, but in the background." Instead of playing something familiar, she leaned into reverent improvisation.

She said, "Technically, it was extremely simple. I played a three note series. Then allowed for silence. Then another three notes, extending into longer winding patterns, always followed by an equal space of silence, and interspersed occasionally with the three-note motif. The music flowed and seemed to play itself. The notes just happened in a melodic pattern. I left silences between each little pattern, and I sometimes repeated the little pattern. I just kept doing that."

Pam reported she wasn't nervous as she played for about 10 minutes. She was playing in memory of her friend who wasn't there anymore. After the event, Pam received many compliments; the very best one was when one woman said to her, "Thank you for setting the space for us."

Pam reflected, "Because it was a grief circle, that's what I was hoping it would do. It got everybody ready for what was coming."

After the event, having tried this new approach, Pam reflected on how it felt for her, "It felt wonderful! It just felt so natural and free, because I wasn't trying to play a song. I was just playing from my heart to theirs and it was a wonderful feeling. I'd like to find more opportunities."

What gave her the courage to play in public once again? Pam answered, "It was a grief circle for a close friend, and I wanted to do something for her. It was just for our group and in memory of a beloved member. I was inspired to be in service. I would love to do it again sometime."

Pam continued, "I don't like to play in front of people, so I don't. I play in the back. I think that gives the music a whole different sound, coming from behind the listeners. And they are not staring at me then. They're only listening and feeling. It has a different effect."

Can you see how this re-orientation of a musician's ego is very different from being a performer? This is often a big shift for people to fully embrace.

As said earlier in the book, your basic musicianship skills need to be in place. What does that look like? If the skill level is low and the musician struggles as they play, it will detract from the ceremony, not enhance it.

The ego of the flute performer must step aside. The breath of the universe plays through you and your flute, in service to the ceremony participants.

The flutes are easy to learn to play and give us a unique ability to tap into the voice of nature, which we know in our bones. But ceremonial playing takes on a new energy. Our direct understanding and embodiment of the ceremony may be new terrain for you, in which case you want to approach this mindfully and respectfully.

Chapter Invitation

1) Musical Breath Mantra

Come to a comfortable position. Bring your focus to your breath. Without changing anything or judging anything, just notice the rise and fall of your breath. [pause] Continue to quiet yourself by slowing and deepening your breath. Sink into a quiet space within. Feel your breath moving through your body. Tune in to the beating of your heart. Begin inhaling slowly and exhaling even more slowly. Let the words ride on your breath, going in and out.

Slowly **inhale**, "**In service**"

And **exhale** even slower, "**I am hollow**."

Go a little deeper into the stillness by repeating this mantra as your breath rides on the words as you inhale "**In service**" and exhale "**I am hollow**."

2) Meditate in this quiet space for a few minutes [pause]

3) Journaling Prompt

Gently deepen your breath and come back fully to the present space and time.
Take one minute to journal on this prompt:

As I breathed the words, **In service, I am hollow**, *I...*

4) Read what you just wrote

Circle or underline any words or phrases that jump out at you as you read. Maintain a compassionate, curious, and above all, non-judgmental attitude as you read. Look for clues and guideposts. Finally, journal once more reflecting on the words or phrases that jump out at you. Are there any surprises in your journaling?

Know Your Listeners

Soul Songs

*In a soul song
words are unnecessary*

a flute sings

*a feeling rides on the
melodic vibrations*

delivered in silence

*held in love and safety
the finest expression
of humanity in community*

*in harmony together
in harmony together*

Know Your Listeners

The people and intention of the ceremony can serve as guides regarding which flutes to play, what volume to play at, which modes to play, and how to play appropriately.

It is important to steadfastly observe our listeners. Observation skills and intuition provides the input needed to navigate. The idea is to offer a soundscape that people can connect to. We are aligned to the ceremony's intention and your perception of the listeners' state so they can take in the sonic environment we are providing.

For example, imagine playing for a contemplative ceremony, such as a Medicine Wheel walk. It would not make sense to start playing fast-paced, high-pitched sounds with a steady beat. It would make more sense to start with an simple melodic theme, and perhaps in a minor key.

If playing for a Celebration of Life ceremony (as opposed to a funeral), while trying to detect the mood of the event, you might offer a light-hearted major mode played with a simple pattern, always in a duet with silence.

Many times, we have no idea who will attend, especially if it's a public event. But if it is a private event, some useful information may be available to you.

Considerations

What is the purpose of the event?
What is the age range of the participants?
What is the ideal tonal range for these people?
Are the people coming to the ceremony to relieve grief?
Are the people chilling after a hard yoga class in meditation?
Are people in a sweat lodge ceremony hoping for a vision?
What is the best volume level range to use?

For young people, higher-pitched flutes can be more appealing as they are more stimulating.
For older people, lower-pitched flutes are usually appreciated as they are more calming.

Consider the space. Do not overwhelm a space with loud flute playing. If you are playing for people walking a labyrinth, they are probably seeking a contemplative experience and are likely going deep into the recesses of their inner world with each step. Similarly, at the end of a Yoga or T'ai Chi class, at a Reiki share, or in a community acupuncture setting, your best bet is to play low-keyed flutes (nothing higher than an F#), played very slowly, softly, and with generous silences.

Always consider balancing your playing between the enchanting sound of the minor scale and the uplifting sound of the major scale so the ceremony doesn't feel too heavy, especially if you are playing for an extended time.

It is important to stay very present to the attendees and what they may be experiencing. An unpredictable situation may occur that participants may react to, especially if you are playing outdoors. Sometimes a breeze kicks up, and something sails across the scene, or a couple of ravens pass by flapping their powerful wings and calling out messages. Or thunder rumbles, and participants look up to see what the weather is doing.

As described in more detail in the Mileage and Commitment chapter, your ability to sense what works becomes more keen over time, and because you are playing live music, you can always pivot in the moment if you feel it is time to change what you are doing.

Do your best to enhance these unexpected moments and be aware of how they may affect participants. You may be asked to play for a very short amount of time. Never underestimate how powerful the healing sound of the flute is, even when played for just a few minutes. Bring the glory of this beautiful practice to every note.

Story

At my father's funeral, a talented harp player, fellow Certified Music Practitioner, and dear friend, DeLuna played at the wake following the church service. This was a time when family members who hadn't seen each other for years came together. DeLuna's playing held us as emotions were on overdrive, and gave us support for our shared grief. The beautiful harp music soothed us. In this case, the instrument was not a flute, but the same principles apply, as they are also based on providing a healing environment for an event when people consider the big questions of life.

Whatever the ceremony, carefully consider your listeners. Put yourself in their shoes, look through their eyes, and hear through their ears for a moment. Follow your intuition as you take that into your heart. The main focus is to support their process. The greatest service the ceremonial player can provide in those moments has nothing to do with fancy instrumental riffs. Tune in deeply to your listeners and ride the wave of the ceremony's intention.

Play for Beings Other than Humans

My husband and I visited the Grand Canyon. During our visit, we drove to the mules stable to play for them. They are the service animals for the tours that descend into the canyon. These mules are magnificent, powerful beings who deserve a rest after a long, hard day in the Canyon.

Just imagine the mules standing around, nearly motionless. I share this story because it is another opportunity to play in this way, honoring beings and observing their reactions.

First, I stood there, before starting to play, and tuned into these beautiful mules. After a few centering breaths, I played one long note. Immediately, their ears perked up, and a few of them turned their heads toward the sound. Then, several mules turned around and walked over. They wanted to see where the new sound in the environment came from. About a half dozen of them lined up at the fence right where I was standing. Standing in about a four to five foot range of these beautiful mules, I played in a ceremonial way.

Silence was my dance partner as I kept my eyes on the mules. They appeared satisfied to just remain standing there as I played to them. More mules came over. This inter-species event filled my soul.

I played for a while, then it was time to go. I made my playing increasingly sparse. One by one, the mules turned away and walked back to the place they came from.

It was a memorable experience. The universal appeal of the sound of the flute created a moment in life to experience the union with all that is.

Turn your idea of "listeners" upside down. Keep in mind the opportunity to play for one of the elements. Perhaps your listener is a visiting hummingbird. Let your ceremonial playing find the environment you are called to play for. Playing for beings other than humans is a beautiful way to become more aware of the natural world.

Turn your idea of "listeners" upside down. Keep in mind the opportunity to play for the elements such as the wind, fire, water, and earth. Perhaps your listener is a visiting hummingbird. Let your ceremonial playing reflect the environment you are called to play for.

Make it a habit to take a flute or two with you when you go out. You may suddenly come across an opportunity to bring your beautiful sound into the world.

Whether your listener is the river, a group at a church service, or any other variations, keep the listeners' focus front and center and remove yourself as the focal point if possible.

In summary, use your observation skills and intuition so your listeners can connect with the soundscape you are offering and go from there. Do your research ahead of the ceremony regarding the demographics. While playing, do your best to watch their responses as you play.

Chapter Invitation

1) Musical Breath Mantra

Come to a comfortable position. Bring your focus to your breath. Without changing anything or judging anything, just notice the rise and fall of your breath. [pause] Continue to quiet yourself by slowing and deepening your breath. Sink into a quiet space within. Feel your breath moving through your body. Tune in to the beating of your heart. Begin inhaling slowly and exhaling even more slowly. Let the words ride on your breath, going in and out.

Slowly **inhale**, "**I play for**"

And **exhale** even slower, "**my listeners.**"

Go a little deeper into the stillness by repeating this mantra as your breath rides on the words as you inhale "**I play for**" and exhale "**my listeners.**"

2) Meditate in this quiet space for a few minutes [pause]

3) Journaling Prompt

Gently deepen your breath and come back fully to the present space and time.
Take one minute to journal on this prompt:

*As I breathed the words, **I play for my listeners**, I imagined them to be…*

4) Read what you just wrote

Circle or underline any words or phrases that jump out at you as you read. Maintain a compassionate, curious, and above all, non-judgmental attitude as you read. Look for clues and guideposts. Finally, journal once more reflecting on the words or phrases that jump out at you. Are there any surprises in your journaling?

Musical Modes Simplified

This Chapter is Optional

All you need to know are these two pentatonic scales shown below, which use the same notes. This is the beauty and power of music. Using these two pentatonic modes, one being the minor pentatonic scale by starting from the bottom hole, and the other being the major pentatonic scale by starting on the 2nd hole up. With these two pentatonic scales, you have everything you need to do this work and you can bypass this chapter. When you want more options with your sound, you can return to this chapter and add a mode. *** indicates pentatonic interval.**

The Pentatonic Minor

🔵 Notice the 3rd and 7th intervals belong to the minor scale.
Also notice the two open spaces where other intervals of the full scale would be.

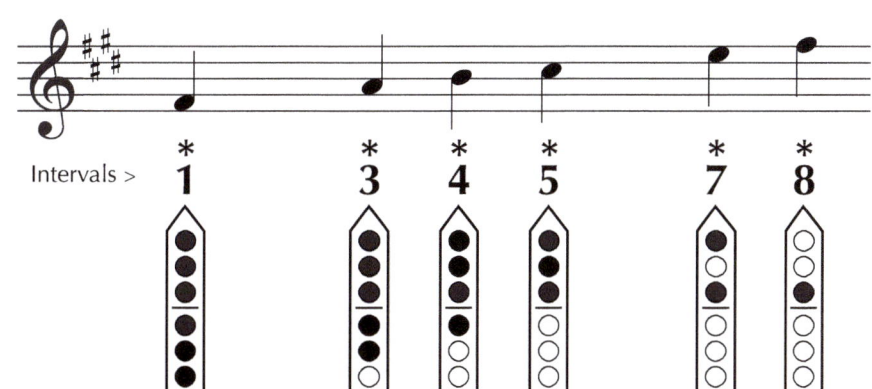

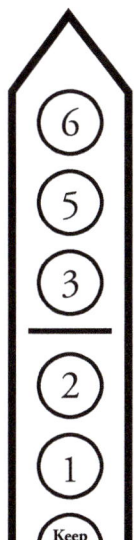

The Pentatonic Major

Notice the two open spaces where other intervals of the full scale would be.

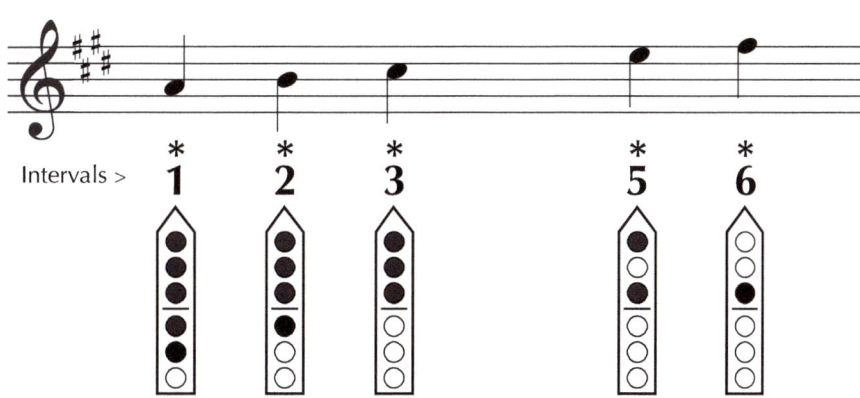

The Modes Simplified

Musical Modes? What are those? It sounds complicated. Does that relate to major and minor? What's the difference? Until now, the modes were a little out of reach for most NAF players. No longer. The material in this chapter helps you broaden your horizons musically. The modes are powerful and have been around for a very long time for many reasons.

The NAF is built on the Aeolian mode (natural minor scale). To get familiar with the chart, see the Aeolian mode, with pentatonic intervals highlighted. This pentatonic scale is typically the first scale learned on the NAF. Pay attention to the * above some of the intervals. The * indicate the **pentatonic** intervals of each mode. You don't have to learn the entire mode if you don't want to. You can just play the pentatonic intervals to get the simplified, essential sound of the mode.

Use the Cheat Sheet and Play the Modes

Play each mode from the illustrations provided on the following pages. You don't have to understand the theory of modes—just play through each mode slowly. Pick one or two that appeal to you and presto!—you've greatly expanded your sound. The "cheat sheet" provided here shows only one fingering option in this book. I have chosen the easiest fingering for each mode, however you can play them starting on other holes.

Recommendation

Balance your sound by using both major and minor modes, weaving them together in a seamless flow with thoughtful transitions.

A Deep Dive is Available

In my book and recorded course, *Discover the Musical Modes on the Native American Style Flute*, each mode is explained thoroughly and illustrated in three positions. It is a deep dive, and you can get all the information about musical modes there.

Some of the Modes Have a Flavor Note

The interval that gives each mode its unique, distinctive sound is color-coded, bold, and has this special asterisk above it: ✺

In this example, the Dorian mode is used. Its distinctive **flavor note**, which differs from mode to mode, is the raised 6th interval. This note gives the Dorian mode its **unique sound**.

As you learn the mode, explore this particular interval. Get familiar with the sound of the mode and how the **flavor note** interval influences the other intervals.

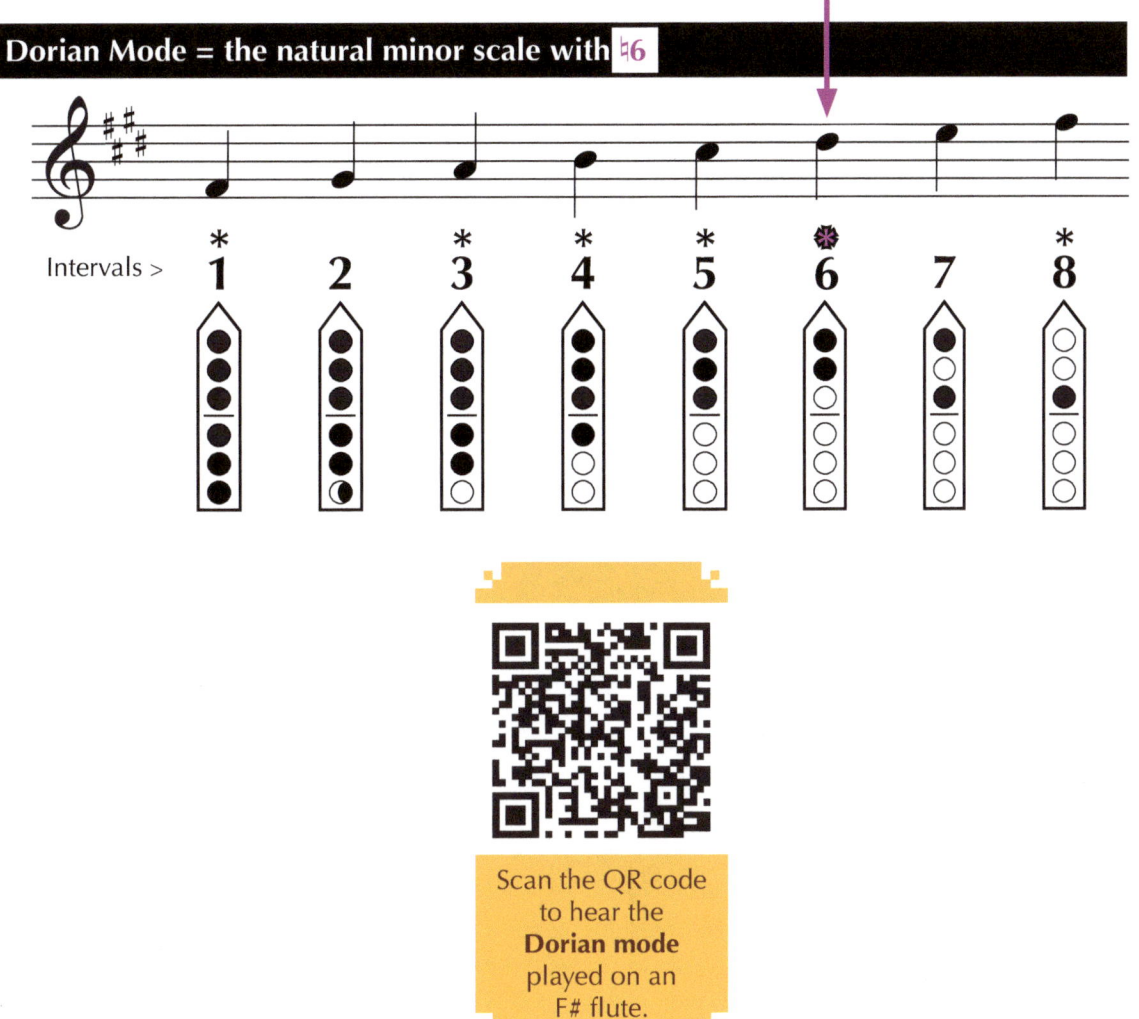

Scan the QR code to hear the **Dorian mode** played on an F# flute.

Major Modes

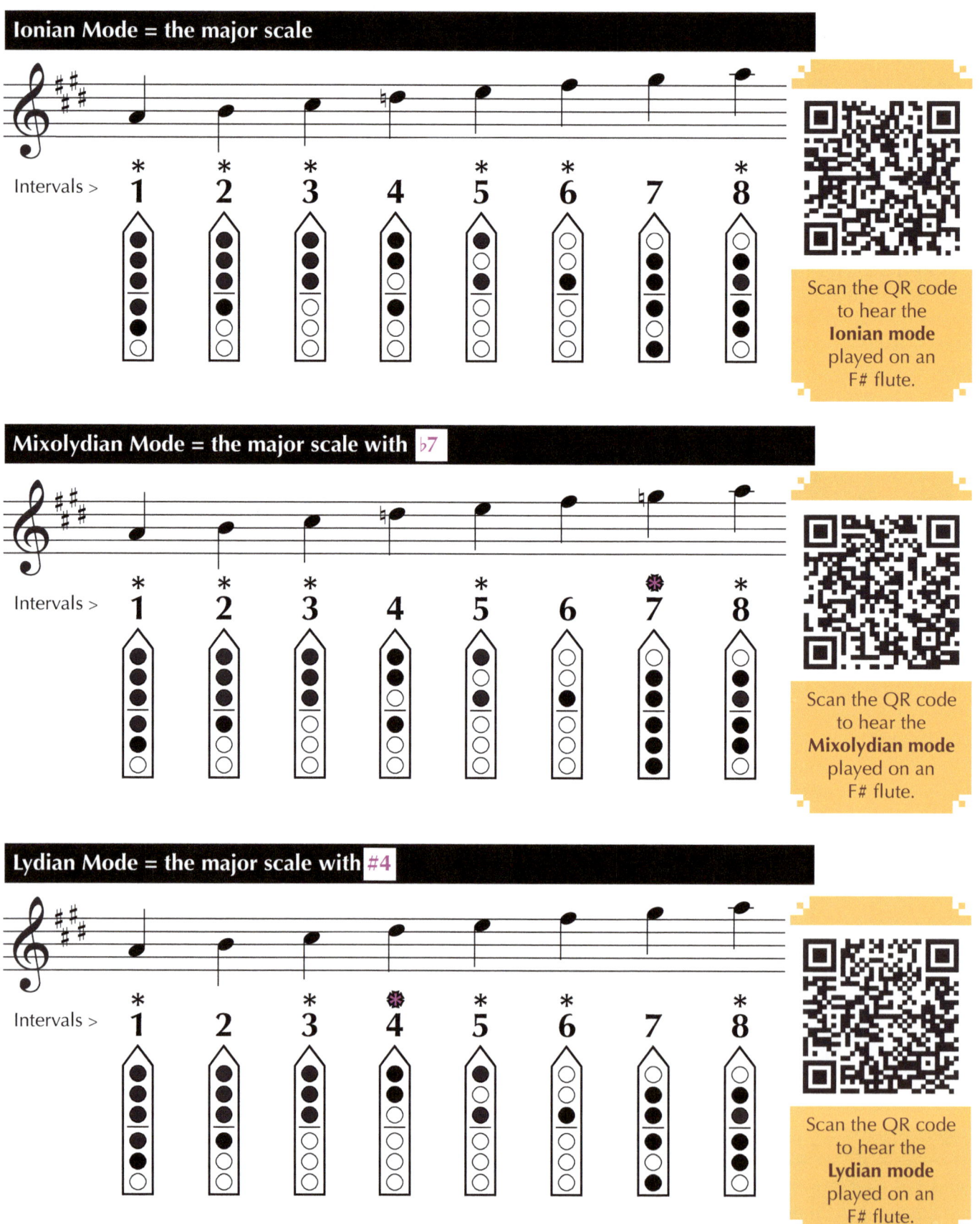

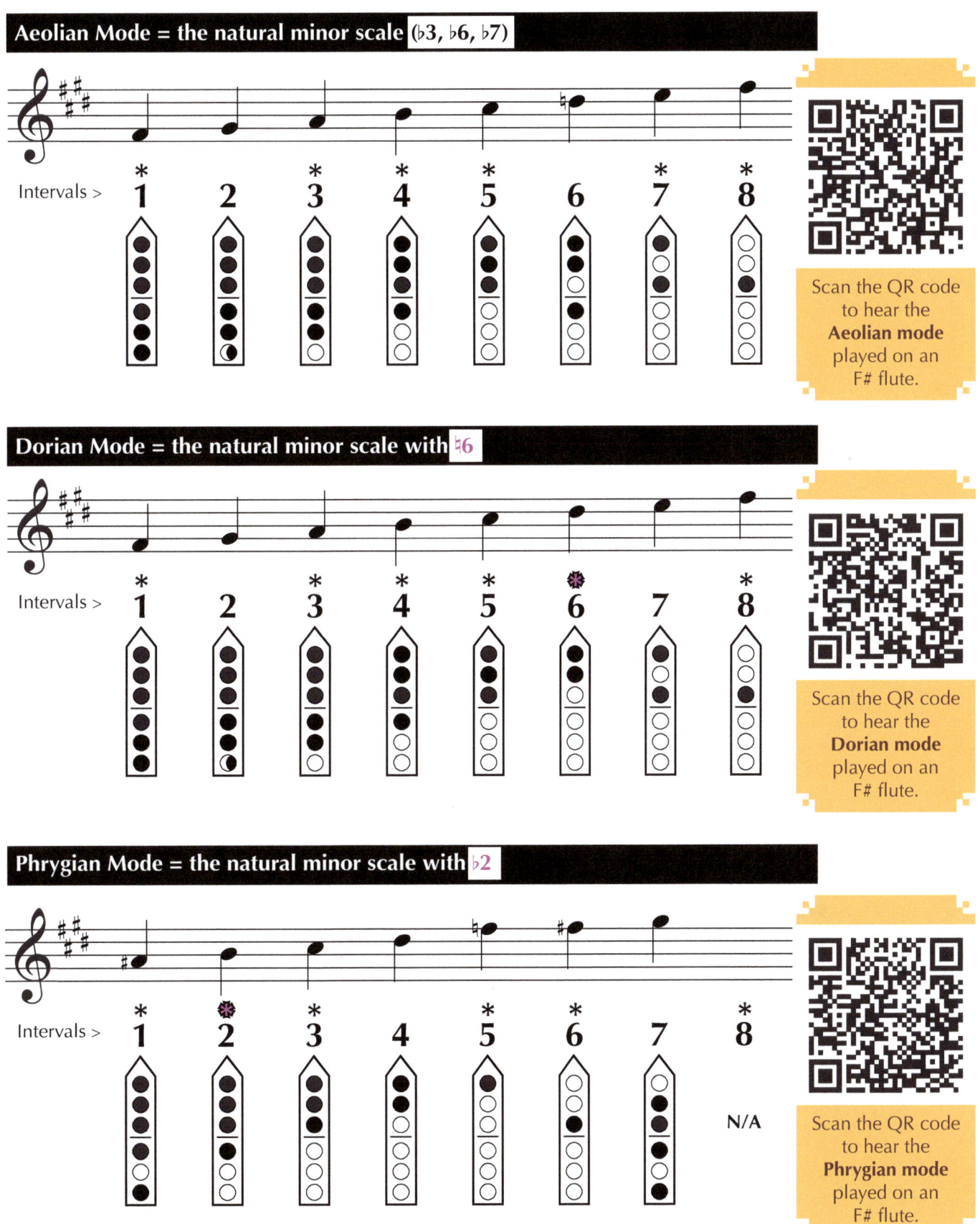

Phrygian Dominant (or Phrygian major)

This provocative mode is also known as the **Ahava Rabbah scale** (used in Hebrew prayers), **Freygish**, **Maqam Hijaz**, and simply, the "Jewish scale" to some. It is identical to Phrygian except for the 3rd interval. From 2 to 3 is a **dramatic whole + half-step!** This whole + half-step jump distinguishes itself from other modes in this book and reveals its **exotic** nature. Lean heavily on the dramatic 3rd. It is highlighted with a red * and is an **important melody note**.

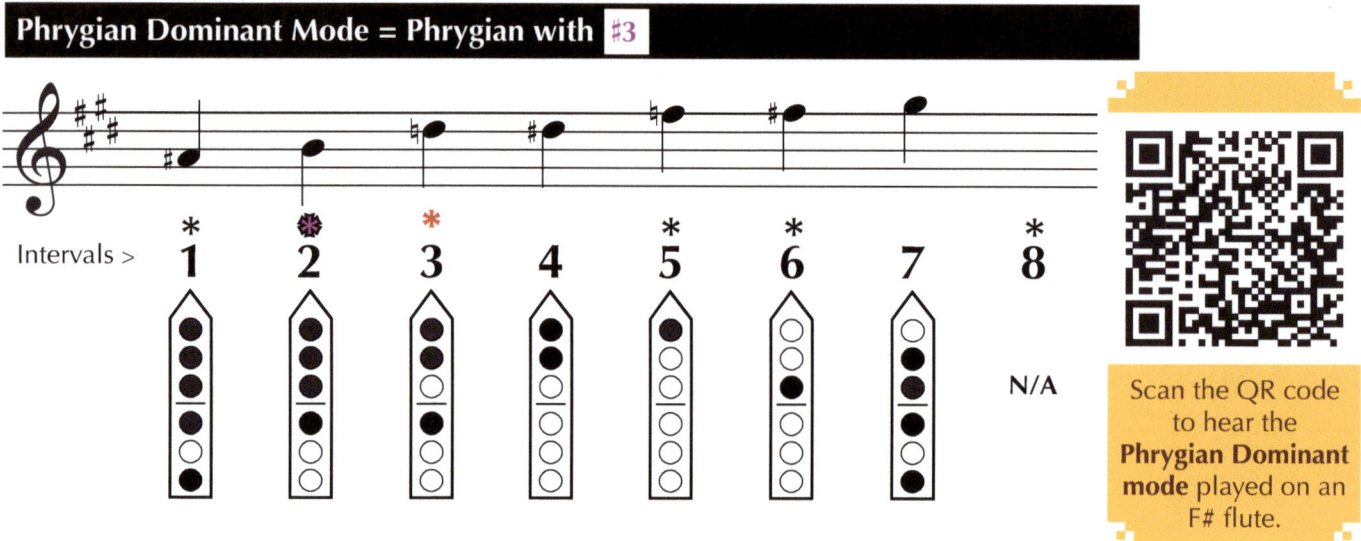

Scan the QR code to hear the **Phrygian Dominant mode** played on an F# flute.

Locrian

Often excluded from modal music because of the unsettling quality of the flatted 5th interval, Locrian offers an unusual sound. Played with an open mind, it could be likened to wind chimes. No sound file or video here, but play through it and listen to its sound.

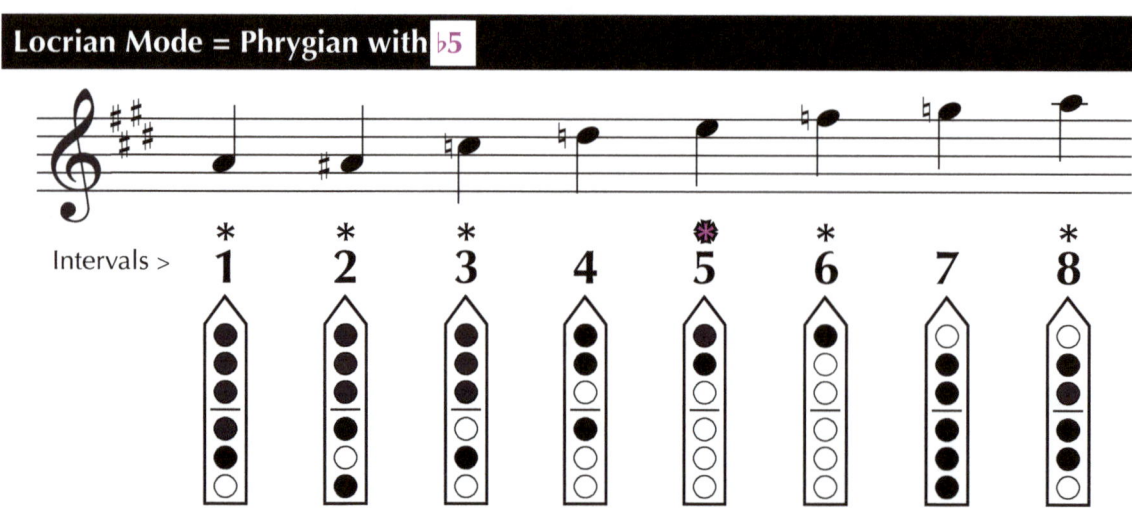

Miyako Bushi Scale

This beautiful scale transports us to a Zen rock garden just as the cherry blossoms are full and exquisite. No sound file or video here, but play through it and listen to its exotic sound.

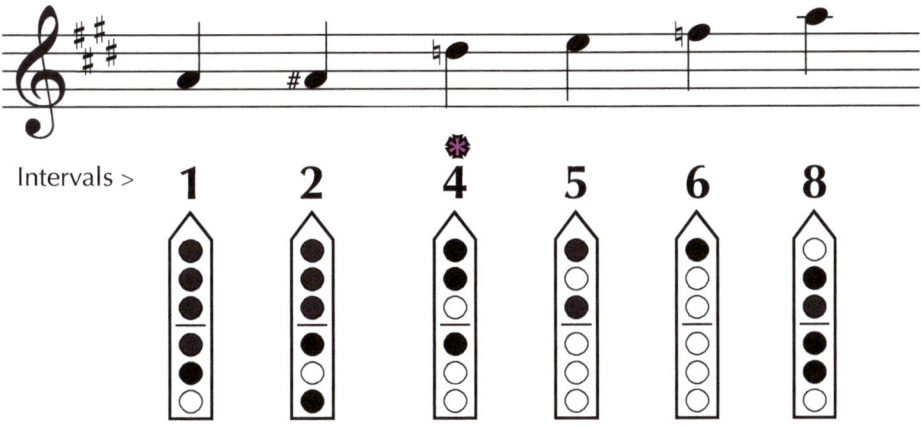

To study music, we must learn the rules. To create music, we must break them.

\- Nadia Boulanger

Chapter Invitation

1) Musical Breath Mantra

Come to a comfortable position. Bring your focus to your breath. Without changing anything or judging anything, just notice the rise and fall of your breath. [pause] Continue to quiet yourself by slowing and deepening your breath. Sink into a quiet space within. Feel your breath moving through your body. Tune in to the beating of your heart. Begin inhaling slowly and exhaling even more slowly. Let the words ride on your breath, going in and out.

Slowly **inhale**, "**I can learn**"

And **exhale** even slower, "**a mode or two.**"

Go a little deeper into the stillness by repeating this mantra as your breath rides on the words as you inhale "**I can learn**" and exhale "**a mode or two.**"

2) Meditate in this quiet space for a few minutes [pause]

3) Journaling Prompt

Gently deepen your breath and come back fully to the present space and time.
Take one minute to journal on this prompt:

As I breathed the words, **I can learn a mode or two**, *I felt confident that…*

4) Read what you just wrote

Circle or underline any words or phrases that jump out at you as you read. Maintain a compassionate, curious, and above all, non-judgmental attitude as you read. Look for clues and guideposts. Finally, journal once more reflecting on the words or phrases that jump out at you. Are there any surprises in your journaling?

Rhythms

Lyrical Dance

*The dance begins
marked by the dancer
in the space between
their feet and the floor*

*a lyrical dance
of paisley patterns
of big and small
of short and long
of simple and fancy
of rising and falling
of high and low*

*the powerful silence between
each choreographed sequence
remains unmeasured*

*intended yet free
a moment like no other
a lyrical dance
poetry in motion
poetry in motion*

Rhythms

Understand Entrainment

Entrainment is the natural tendency for a listener's internal rhythms, such as heart rate, respiratory rate, and motor movement, to synchronize with an external rhythm source, such as drumming or playing a flute at a certain pace. An example of entrainment is when you listen to music and tap your foot almost automatically. The rest of the body follows. Your heart rate will start to sync with the rhythmic pace of the music. Through your ears and skin, an entire network is activated, affecting every system in your body. Just listen to a song you love that has a strong rhythm and try not to move. You'll surely experience the body rebelling against its natural inclination to entrain to what it is hearing.

Entrainment falls under the category of rhythm in the overall elements of music. Rhythm is one of music's many superpowers. Why? Entrainment to rhythm is a natural response. When exposed to an external sound, a cascade of events occurs in the human system. It cannot be overemphasized. It is worth taking some time to understand the physics of entrainment through a self-directed study.

Here is a brief framework to quickly grasp the magnitude and potential of music's superpower through entrainment. It is essential to understand how your flute music affects listeners. Every ear will receive the sound. Even in cases of hearing loss, the vibrations still reach other sensory systems, such as the body's biggest ear, the skin. The sounds in our environment affect us on physical, mental, emotional, and spiritual levels. It is important that you know what you're doing as the musician. If the goal is to play for a contemplative effect, the rhythm patterns offered below will give you an instant framework.

Simple Patterns

Nature is made up of patterns. We love patterns. The simple patterns provided in this chapter provide a fast on-ramp to ceremonial playing and can be used in patterns as you get masterful at them. We want people to experience the ceremony, and if we play anything complex, using too many notes, it will only be distracting. Knowing what happens automatically through the principle of entrainment, here are simple rhythmic patterns that will be the framework for this style.

How to Slow People Down

Here is an example of how to use ceremonial playing to gently move people into a gradually slower pace.

Short **LONG** is the bedrock rhythm concept used in this style of playing. There are several variations, but the concept of *short* **LONG** is what we're going to work with first.

Exercise:

Play *short* **LONG** three times using any note and stretch the timeline by playing it more slowly each time you play.

The first time you play, make the *short* **LONG** rhythm pattern span about 5 seconds.

Play it again, but draw it out longer. There's no need to get too mathematical about this. No need to count, just make it relatively longer and trust yourself.

Play *short* **LONG** again, but this time, make it last even longer. Breath whenever you want to. Stop counting. Just extend time. Slow it down. This slowing down entrainment technique helps move listeners into a slower pace.

Just to acknowledge, in a shamanic journey, a different kind of ceremony, the practitioner would certainly play a very fast, even pace on a drum or other percussion instrument so people could achieve a theta brainwave state. That is definitely ceremonial playing, but of a different element. Notice that the practice of entrainment also shows up in this example.

What is being recommended here is avoiding a steady beat that would cause your listeners to entrain to a march step pattern. Instead, this style of playing encourages a dreamlike, ethereal atmosphere. For that effect, very loose timing is used. No time signatures. Just the idea of *short* and **LONG**. Every combination works and all musical phrases finish with **LONG**.

Four Simple Rhythmic Patterns

Use **only one note** as you play these rhythms. Trust your intuition regarding short and long. Short is about one beat. Don't overthink it. Play one rhythmic pattern per breath, followed by silence. Play each pattern using only one note so you can easily internalize each rhythm. Ride the breath. Follow each phrase with silence.

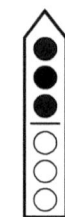

1 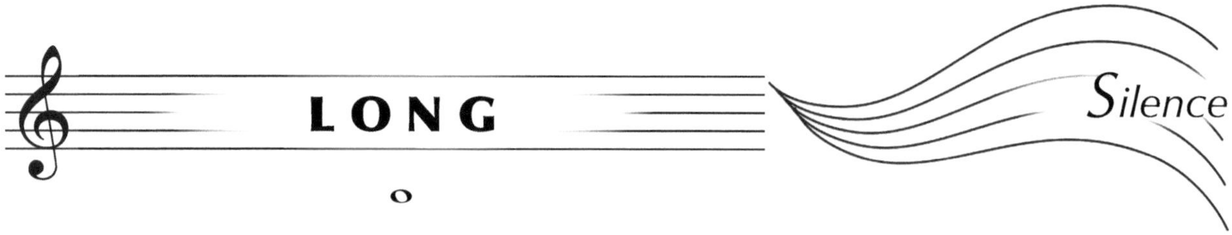 LONG — Silence

2 short LONG — Silence

3 short short LONG — Silence

4 LONG LONG — Silence

Shown Differently

Try the four rhythms again using this visual. Again, try out each pattern using only one note so you can easily internalize each rhythm. There is a universe in every note. Make each note come alive through your breath.

To begin, use **only one note** as you play these rhythms.

Rhythmic Pattern #1: **L O N G**

Ride the breath. There is a universe in every note.
Play one rhythmic pattern per breath, then *Silence*...

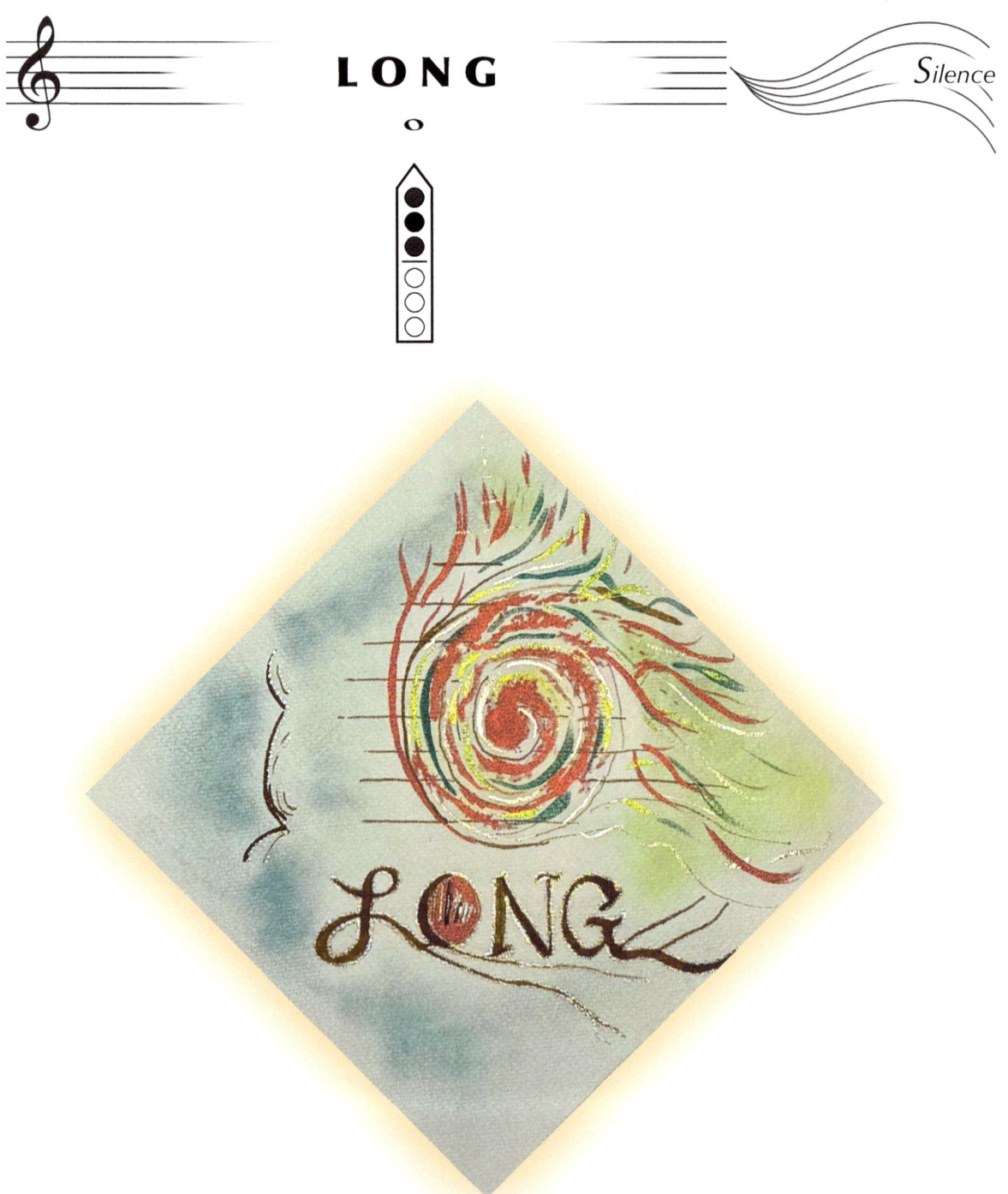

Rhythmic Pattern #2: short **L O N G**

Ride the breath. There is a universe in every note.
Play one rhythmic pattern per breath, then *Silence*...

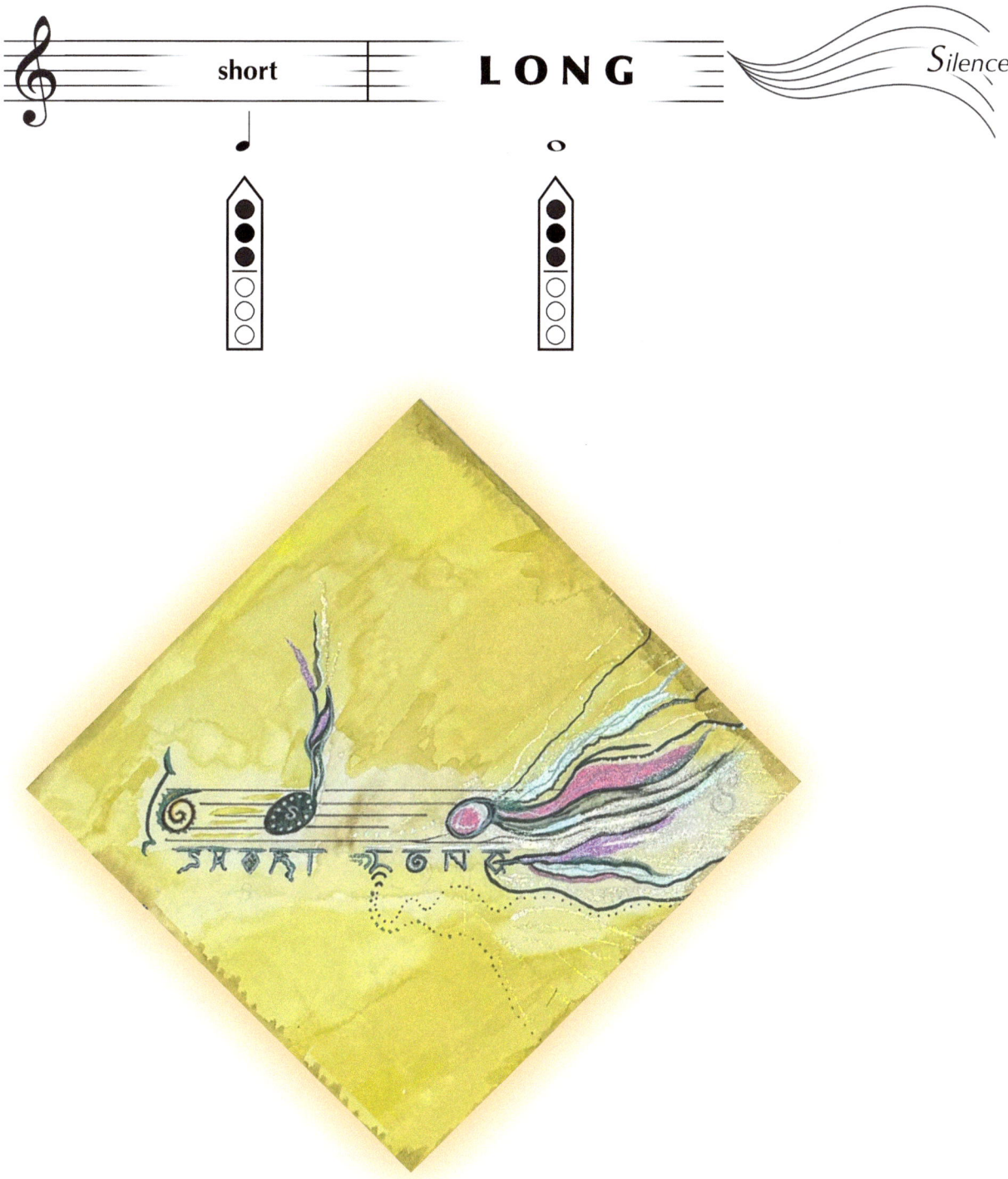

Rhythmic Pattern #3: short short **L O N G**

Ride the breath. There is a universe in every note.
Play one rhythmic pattern per breath, then *Silence...*

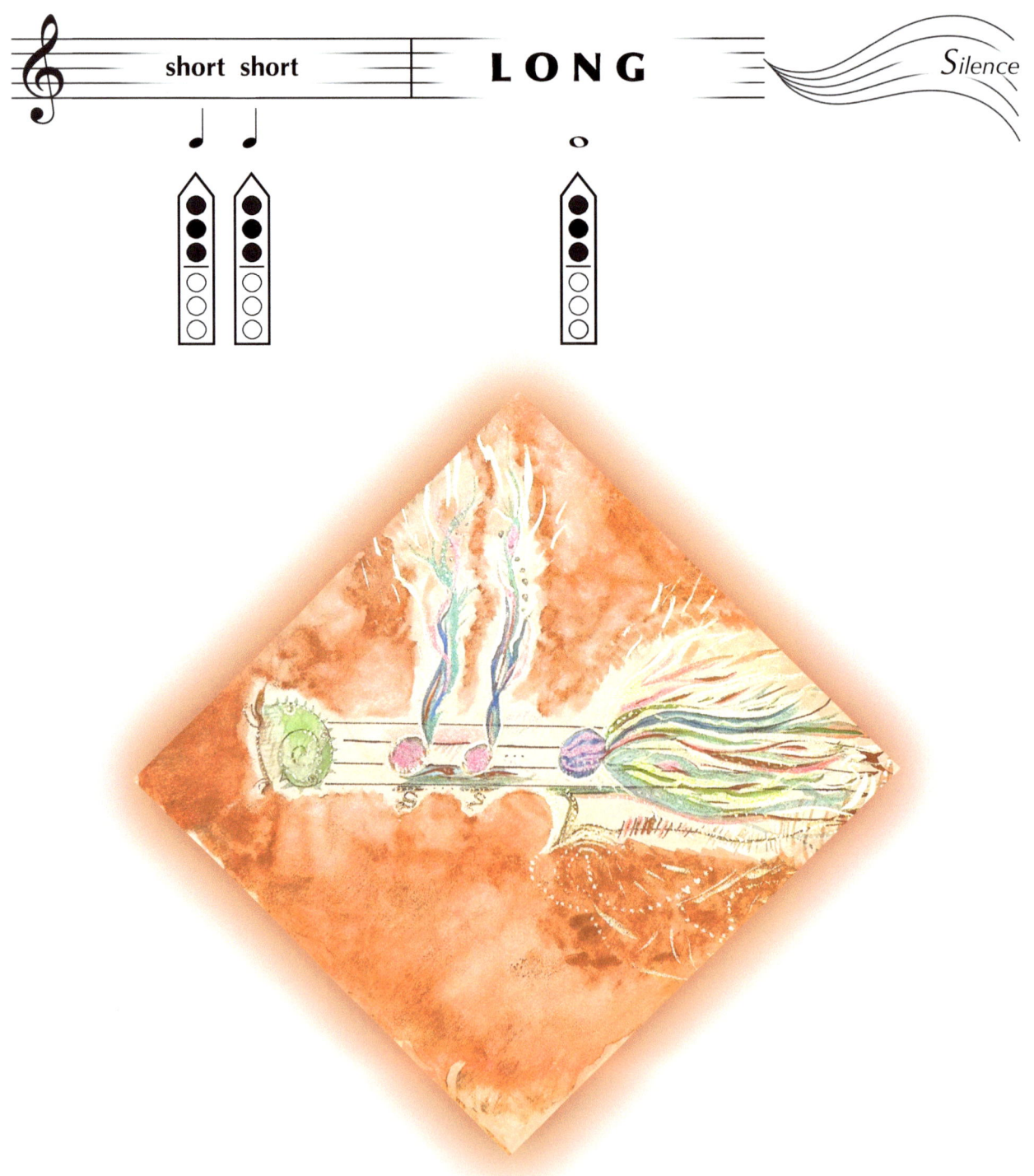

Rhythmic Pattern #4: **LONG LONG**

Ride the breath. There is a universe in every note.
Play one rhythmic pattern per breath, then *Silence*...

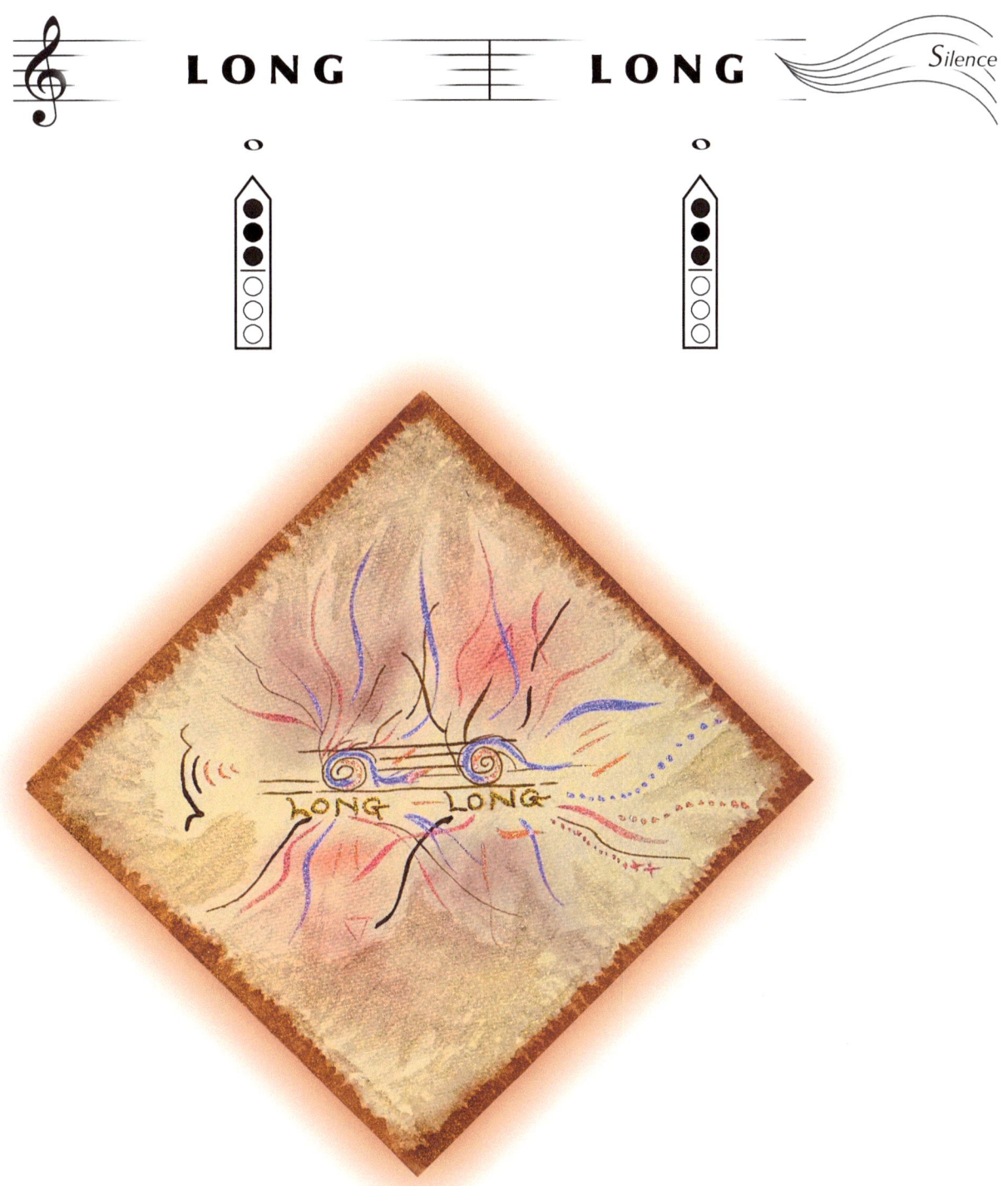

Chapter Invitation

1) Musical Breath Mantra

Come to a comfortable position. Bring your focus to your breath. Without changing anything or judging anything, just notice the rise and fall of your breath. [pause] Continue to quiet yourself by slowing and deepening your breath. Sink into a quiet space within. Feel your breath moving through your body. Tune in to the beating of your heart. Begin inhaling slowly and exhaling even more slowly. Let the words ride on your breath, going in and out.

Slowly *inhale*, "**The rhythm**"

And *exhale* even slower, "**sets the whole pace.**"

Go a little deeper into the stillness by repeating this mantra as your breath rides on the words as you inhale **"the rhythm"** and exhale "**sets the whole pace.**"

2) Meditate in this quiet space for a few minutes [pause]

3) Journaling Prompt

Gently deepen your breath and come back fully to the present space and time. Take one minute to journal on this prompt:

As I breathed the words, **the rhythm sets the whole pace**, *I imagined...*

4) Read what you just wrote

Circle or underline any words or phrases that jump out at you as you read. Maintain a compassionate, curious, and above all, non-judgmental attitude as you read. Look for clues and guideposts. Finally, journal once more reflecting on the words or phrases that jump out at you. Are there any surprises in your journaling?

The Phenomenal Breath

The breath is the domain where we make the ceremonial flute playing phenomenal.

Ami Sarasvati

The Phenomenal Breath

The breath is the power source of the flute. No breath, no sound. But especially on the NAF, the breath is more significant than just the required power source. The breath is the domain where we make the ceremonial playing on the NAF phenomenal.

Due to the unique ability of the NAF to showcase breath articulations and nuances, fluency with breath techniques is foundational. To express oneself creatively with the breath is a vital component of artistry. With a command of the breath, we can create a rich sonic experience.

The phenomenal breath has texture. The constant variation of the breath, played intuitively, is the hallmark of this instrument. Even if you just play one note, play it beautifully. Explore and celebrate it. Take flight on every breath.

Notice the textures and overtones of this bio-acoustic sample of a Swift (*Apus apus*) vocalization.

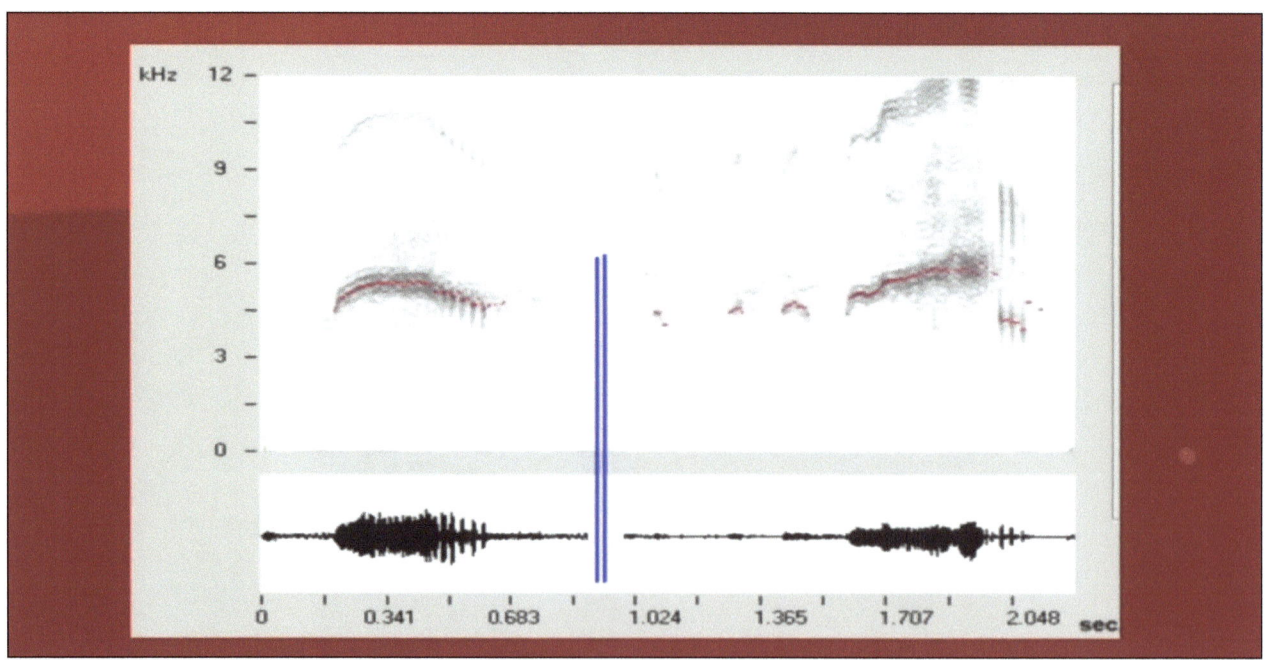

With permission by Marco Dragonetti - www.birdsongs.it

Get inspired by nature in its raw expression as seen by this bio-acoustic sample! Develop your signature style by fluctuating the breath, adding nuanced textures for a phenomenal sound. Your unique sonic ability is as unique as your fingerprint. No one else can make your sound. Use these ideas to create your one-of-a-kind musical alchemy.

The phenomenal breath is where musical alchemy happens. The breath is the elusive magician who alchemizes the notes, the pace, the silence, the intent, the microtones, and the numerous textural possibilities with each breath.

Use your intuition to create a soul-stirring, ceremonial atmosphere, partner with silence that touches the mind, body, and soul of the listeners.

Create Texture with Your Breath

Imagine yourself as a bird and flap your wings through your breath! Take all your passion and visualize yourself shaking the walls of a cave. May your breath always be creating texture like the Swift's song.

What else can we do with the phenomenal breath? One of my favorite features of the NAF is that we can elevate the pitch with more breath and flatten the pitch with less breath. This allows us

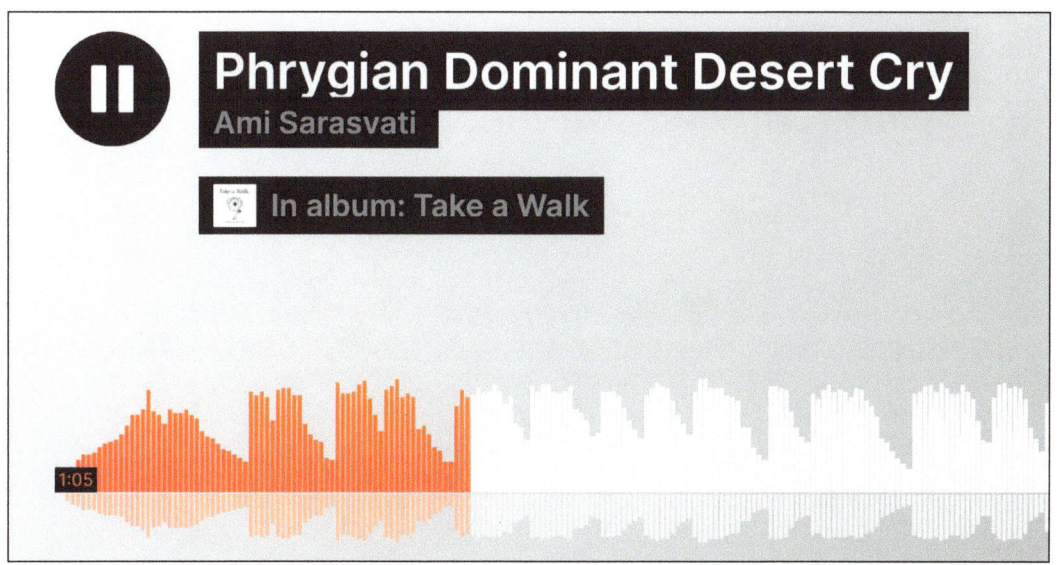

to increase and decrease the pitch on any note. Use a tuner and watch what happens as you vary your breath while playing one note on the flute. Try each note by itself and see how high and low of a pitch you can get with each note. Use pitch bending, subtle rhythm techniques, vibrato, and silence. The technique of pitch bending allows us to play microtones on the flutes.

Use a digital voice recorder or an app like Voice Memos to record yourself playing. On the recording, take a look at the shape of your sound clip. Recording yourself will accelerate your awareness of the texture of your breath. Experiment with making textures that you can see on the recording. Stick with one note. The idea is to develop your understanding of more or less breath volume, and how that shapes your sound. There is even an element of rhythm in your pulsing breath, which subtly shares the same abilities as the entrainment principles.

Imagine the picture of a sound clip. Steady sound makes a flatter line. Textured sound makes shapes. Shapes and silence are what we're after in a recording and in our playing.

How can you use the breath

more consciously

to create texture

and emotion?

Arcing Notes

By constantly and intuitively varying the breath as you play, aim to play each note with an arc shape. You enter the note at its sweet spot, and then slightly energize it with more breath then return to the sweet spot. By using this concept, we avoid playing notes that are simply sounds coming from our flutes, with no dimension or texture.

Make your playing COME ALIVE! with the phenomenal breath!

Add Dimension and Texture to All Notes

Breath techniques to continually develop and refine are:

- Breath volume variations
- Subtle and not-so-subtle pulsing with the breath
- Vibrato at slow, medium, and fast speeds
- Aim to arc each note

Chapter Invitation

1) Musical Breath Mantra

Come to a comfortable position. Bring your focus to your breath. Without changing anything or judging anything, just notice the rise and fall of your breath. [pause] Continue to quiet yourself by slowing and deepening your breath. Sink into a quiet space within. Feel your breath moving through your body. Tune in to the beating of your heart. Begin inhaling slowly and exhaling even more slowly. Let the words ride on your breath, going in and out.

Slowly *inhale*, "**With the breath**"

And *exhale* even slower, "**I exhale clouds**."

Go a little deeper into the stillness by repeating this mantra as your breath rides on the words as you inhale "**With the breath**" and exhale "**I exhale clouds**."

2) Meditate in this quiet space for a few minutes [pause]

3) Journaling Prompt

Gently deepen your breath and come back fully to the present space and time. Take one minute to journal on this prompt:

As I breathed the words, **With the breath, I exhale clouds**, *I felt confident that...*

4) Read what you just wrote

Circle or underline any words or phrases that jump out at you as you read. Maintain a compassionate, curious, and above all, non-judgmental attitude as you read. Look for clues and guideposts. Finally, journal once more reflecting on the words or phrases that jump out at you. Are there any surprises in your journaling?

Simple Melodic Phrases

The Composition

A fine gift
arrives in a flash

with no effort asked
but the quick hand
of the scribe

listening carefully
to the miraculous arrival

heralding a fine gift
arriving with clarity

and disappearing

into the mystery
into the mystery

Simple Melodic Phrases

When creating simple melodic phrases, any of the rhythm patterns in the wheel below work well. Any pattern *next to* any other pattern works.

Always return to the center where *silence* has its turn.
Patterns can be repeated. Play simple patterns using this wheel.

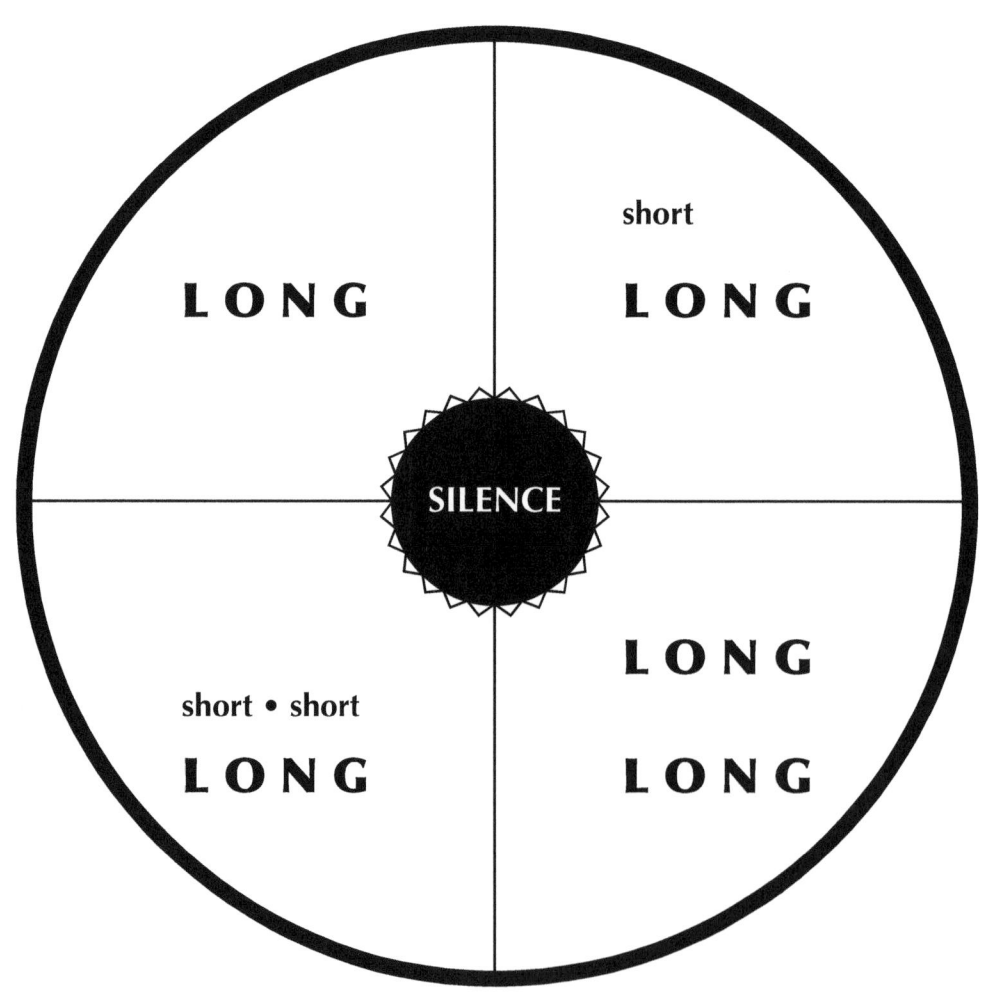

Two-Voice Development Process

Notice the ovals around the intervals 4 & 5, and another around 5, 7, & 8. The ovals represent **voices**. **Voices** are simply a few intervals chosen to create a mini-melody. A second voice emerges as a companion to the first voice. The two voices often share one interval.

1) Choose a scale or mode (example pentatonic minor)

2) Establish the tonal center
Playing the 1st interval of the scale or mode.

3) Pick two more intervals
Voice 1   Example: 4 5
Those intervals will be dance partners.

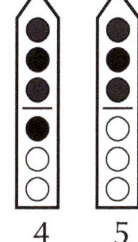

4) Pick two or three more intervals
Voice 2   Example: 5 7 8
Those intervals will be dance partners.
Meander as you develop Voice 2.
Keep it simple. Use these patterns masterfully.

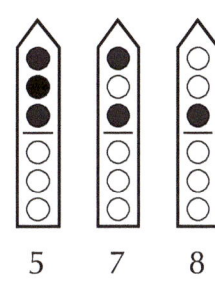

5) Dance between the voices and silence
Repeat and reflect themes back and forth as you like. Make it come alive with vibrato and vary the breath on every note.
Use ornaments, but keep it subtle. Watch for playing too many notes in one breath.
The strength of the flute is its simplicity and the sublime tone the NAF produces when we use the phenomenal breath while playing.

6) Simplify and resolve to interval 1 (the home note)

Scan the QR code and follow along to Example #1

Recorded on D flute using pentatonic minor scale.
Listen to the pace and use of silence.

Example #1:

Establish the tonal center (1) then develop the first voice of the story made up of intervals 4 & 5.

1

Scan the QR code to hear **Example #1** played on a D flute.

short	short	LONG (followed by silence)
-	-	1 (establish tonal center)
	1	5
5	4	5
	5	4
	5	5
Repeat once from beginning, then:		
5	4	4
4	5	5
-	4	4
-	5	5

Voice 2: Using intervals 5, 7, & 8

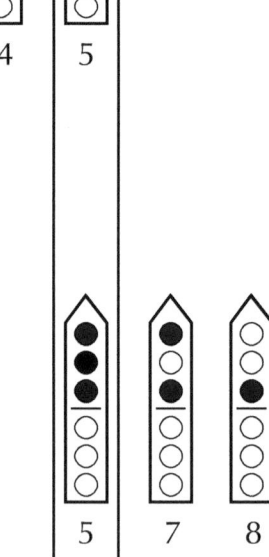

short	short	LONG (followed by silence)
5	7	5
5	7	5 (slower)
7	5	5
-	7	5
-	-	5
Repeat Voice 2 thus far		
Add the 8		
5	8	7
8	7	5
8	7	7
7	5	5

Voice 1 and Voice 2 Interplay

short	short	LONG (followed by silence)
5	4	4
8	7	5
4	5	5
7	8	7
5	4	4
8	7	7
5	5	5
-	4	4
-	7	5
-	5	4
7	5	5
4	4	5
5	7	5
4	4	5
Then simplify and resolve.		
-	4	5
-	5	5
7	5	5
5	4	4
5	1	1
-	1	1

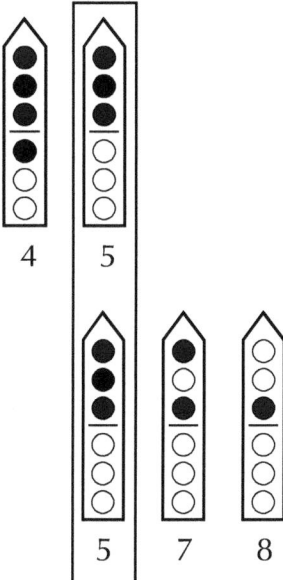

Voice 1 and Voice 2 Alternatives

Voice 1 can have three intervals, and Voice 2 can have two. They can both have two or three. Keep it no more than three intervals per voice and aim to have only two intervals in one of the voices. Asymmetry is a favorable quality and creates interest. Open to your intuitive nature and keep it simple. Use lots of silence between phrases.

Scan the QR code and follow along to Example #2

Recorded on D flute using pentatonic minor scale.

Listen to the pace and use of silence.

Example #2:

Play the tonal center (1) then develop:

Voice 1: use intervals 3 & 4

short	short	LONG (followed by silence)
-	-	1 (establish tonal center)
	1	3
4	3	4
	4	3
	3	4
Repeat once from beginning, then:		
-	4	4
3	4	4
4	3	3
-	3	4

Voice 2: use intervals 4, 5 & 7

short	short	LONG (followed by silence)
4	5	5
5	4	5
5	4	4
-	-	4
-	-	5
Repeat Voice 2 thus far.		
Add the 7		
4	5	7
7	5	4
7	5	5
5	4	4

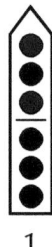

Scan the QR code to hear **Example #2** played on a D flute.

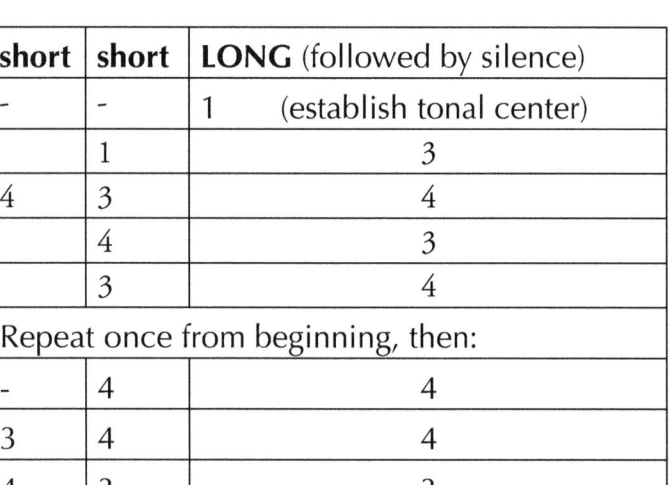

Voice 1 and Voice 2 Interplay

short	short	LONG (followed by silence)
5	4	4
7	5	5
4	5	5
7	5	7
5	4	4
5	7	7
5	5	5
-	4	4
-	7	5
-	5	4
7	5	5
4	4	5
5	7	5
4	4	4
Then simplify and resolve.		
-	4	5
-	5	5
7	5	5
5	4	4
5	1	1
-	1	1

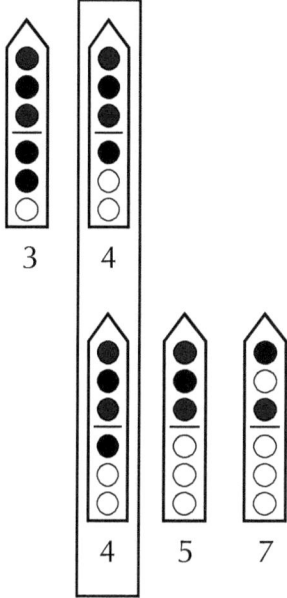

Scan the QR code and follow along to Example #3

Recorded on D flute using pentatonic minor scale.
Listen to the pace and use of silence.

Example #3:
Turn it upside down and start from the top note!

Develop the first voice of the story made up of intervals 8, 7, & 5.

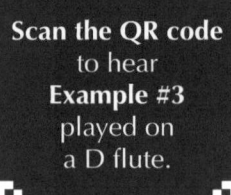

Voice 1: use intervals 8 7 5

short	short	LONG (followed by silence)
-	8	7
8	7	5
7	8	5
	7	5
8	8	7
Repeat once from beginning, then:		
-	7	7
5	7	5
8	8	7
-	7	7

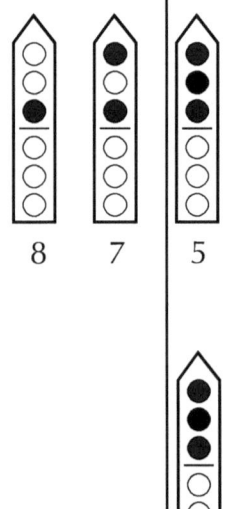

Voice 2: use intervals 5 4

short	short	LONG (followed by silence)
5	4	5
	5	4
	5	5
Repeat once from beginning, then:		
5	4	4
4	5	5
-	4	4
-	5	5

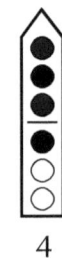

Voice 1 and Voice 2 Interplay

short	short	LONG (followed by silence)
8	7	7
4	5	5
7	5	5
5	4	5
-	7	5
5	7	7
-	-	5
-	5	5
-	-	4
-	-	5
4	5	5
5	7	5
	5	4
-	4	4
Then simplify and resolve.		
8	7	5
5	4	5
7	5	5
-	4	4
8	7	5
-	-	5

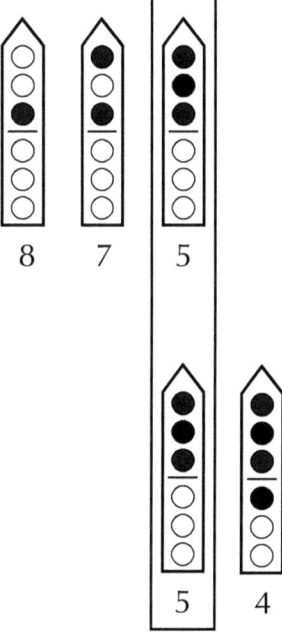

Create Your Own Voice 1 and Voice 2

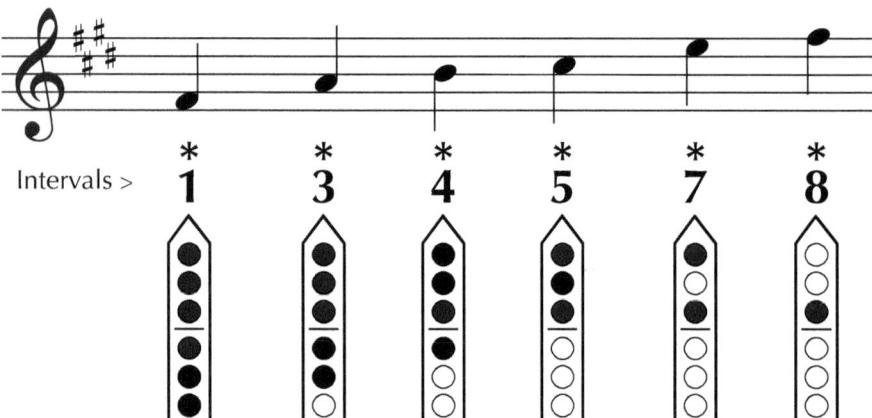

| Intervals > | 1 | 3 | 4 | 5 | 7 | 8 |

Voice 1:

short	short	LONG (then silence)

Voice 1
Choose 2 or 3 intervals from the scale. Draw them in here.

Voice 2: Consider using a common interval from Voice 1.

short	short	LONG (then silence)

Voice 2
Choose 2 or 3 intervals from those above. Draw them in here.

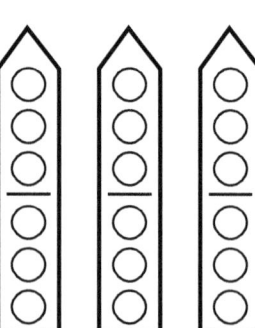

Now let **Voices 1** and **Voice 2** sing.		
short	short	LONG (then silence)
...	...	...
When you're ready, simplify and resolve.		

What's Next? Developing Your Own Signature Sound

This chapter, as well as the *Rhythms* chapter, should be used as **building blocks** that give you a foundation to play in this way.

The simple patterns and ideas are presented as seeds for you to use as presented or as starting points for your own creation. Just remember to keep it very simple and always be in a duet with silence.

Here are two examples of using these ideas, and then going free in expression in the moment. Get inspired and get ready to develop your own unique sound!

Major scale improvisation: **Daydream Stroll**
Listen to the pace and use of silence.
Improvised by the author.

Scan the QR code to hear **Daydream Stroll**.

Minor scale, improvisation: **Moonlight Mood**
Listen to the pace and use of silence.
Improvised by the author.

Scan the QR code to hear **Moonlight Mood**.

www.learntoplayNAF.com

Chapter Invitation

1) Musical Breath Mantra

Come to a comfortable position. Bring your focus to your breath. Without changing anything or judging anything, just notice the rise and fall of your breath. [pause] Continue to quiet yourself by slowing and deepening your breath. Sink into a quiet space within. Feel your breath moving through your body. Tune in to the beating of your heart. Begin inhaling slowly and exhaling even more slowly. Let the words ride on your breath, going in and out.

Slowly **inhale**, "**Two voices**"

And **exhale** even slower, "**gives me balance**."

Go a little deeper into the stillness by repeating this mantra as your breath rides on the words as you inhale "**Two voices**" and exhale "**gives me balance**."

2) Meditate in this quiet space for a few minutes [pause]

3) Journaling Prompt

Gently deepen your breath and come back fully to the present space and time. Take one minute to journal on this prompt:

As I breathed the words, **Two voices gives me balance**, *I realized how ...*

4) Read what you just wrote

Circle or underline any words or phrases that jump out at you as you read. Maintain a compassionate, curious, and above all, non-judgmental attitude as you read. Look for clues and guideposts. Finally, journal once more reflecting on the words or phrases that jump out at you. Are there any surprises in your journaling?

Mileage and Commitment

Go confidently in the direction of your dreams. Live the life you have imagined. As you simplify your life, the laws of the universe will be simpler.

- Henry David Thoreau

There is no substitution for mileage. Any pursuit requires practice of the pursuit itself to achieve competence. We all start exactly where we are and simply get better with each and every try. Don't wait for mastery. Don't worry about mastery. Focus on playing beautifully, with the guidelines from this book in your back pocket, and play with great feeling. Come with a servant's heart, ready and willing to play in service to the ceremony and the participants. Use trial and error, stay compassionate, especially with yourself, and get out there and start playing!

It is easy to get trapped in the cycle of getting ready to get ready to get ready. As long as you have good fluency with the NAF, and you are ready to be of service, you are ready! Mastery follows mileage and commitment.

Training Grounds

It starts with a desire within one's soul. Getting out and playing will lead you step-by-step on this path. Your own backyard will do as a starting point. That's where I started.

When I first bought an NAF, I was living in a 2-family townhouse in Contoocook, NH. That's where my "public" flute playing started. I took my first courageous step when I bought my first NAF from a local flute maker. I had learned a few basics from a couple of books I bought and from videos online. The next day, I was out in the backyard. I played for a few minutes, walking around, and I found a little pattern of notes that was pleasing to me. I just wanted to play them over and over again, and so I did, walking around the yard.

The next day, in the basement doing laundry, my neighbor appeared, who was also doing her laundry. She asked me if I would be playing my flute again soon. She told me she really enjoyed hearing the flute playing the day before. At first, I was concerned that I might have disturbed her, but she expressed only gratitude and encouragement. Not everyone in my life was encouraging, but one kind soul was, so I kept playing.

Unfortunately, family members can be unkind. If you are getting negative feedback from those you live with, don't let them interfere with gaining mileage. Go find somewhere else to play if you need to, but without mileage, you'll literally go nowhere.

Make a plan. Volunteer. Take a few lessons, but find your way into playing for ceremonies with this gorgeous instrument and your healing presence. Create your musical ministry in a way that is unique and rewarding for you.

This book is dedicated to your development as a ceremonial player. Cross the bridge and begin to create your unique sound. Do not be the focal point of the ceremony, but play with the heart of service. Honor your duet with silence for depth and healing. Remember that entrainment is happening, whether you are aware of it or not. Play nothing familiar, but instead improvise with sublime simplicity. The power of the flute is very strong, and your musical ministry awaits you now.

Your Fingerprint

You are one of a kind. The creation of your musical alchemy is yours alone. It is as beautiful and unique as your fingerprint. Mileage will lead you to your signature sound that is unlike anyone else's, and one that only you can make.

What does your unique musical fingerprint look like?

Chapter Invitation

1) Musical Breath Mantra

Come to a comfortable position. Bring your focus to your breath. Without changing anything or judging anything, just notice the rise and fall of your breath. [pause] Continue to quiet yourself by slowing and deepening your breath. Sink into a quiet space within. Feel your breath moving through your body. Tune in to the beating of your heart. Begin inhaling slowly and exhaling even more slowly. Let the words ride on your breath, going in and out.

Slowly *inhale*, "**Only I**"

And *exhale* even slower, "**can make my sound.**"

Go a little deeper into the stillness by repeating this mantra as your breath rides on the words as you inhale "**Only I**" and exhale "**can make my sound.**"

2) Meditate in this quiet space for a few minutes [pause]

3) Journaling Prompt

Gently deepen your breath and come back fully to the present space and time. Take one minute to journal on this prompt:

As I breathed the words, **Only I can make my sound**, *I imagined playing to...*

4) Read what you just wrote

Circle or underline any words or phrases that jump out at you as you read. Maintain a compassionate, curious, and above all, non-judgmental attitude as you read. Look for clues and guideposts. Finally, journal once more reflecting on the words or phrases that jump out at you. Are there any surprises in your journaling?

Appendix

Positions 1, 2, A#, and 3 on the NAF

The flute can be played in a variety of starting notes, here is a chart to explain where those positions are. The following pages are chromatic scales starting from these positions. There is also one more position, A#, that is illustrated as the final possible fingering in this book. This is put in here as Phrygian Dominant, a popular mode, is played starting in the A# position, so for those charting an improvisation, the chromatic scale has a good resource in here to work with.

Starting Positions

Factors to consider when choosing a position:

- How important is the **2nd interval** in the music? If the half-hole is your 2nd interval and played frequently, consider using **Position 2** or **3 instead of Position 1**.

- What is the **highest note** of the music you are going to play? Is it an important note that is **held for a long time**? Is it played **frequently**? Consider the quality of the sound of the note that your flute makes, as well as the importance and frequency of the high note(s).

- Also, consider the music, then decide what position makes the most sense for your flute's range and tonal ability.

- With cross-fingering and some limitations of high notes, you can play the major and minor scales from any of these positions.

Position 1

< **Start on the 1st hole.**

Position 2

< **Start on the 2nd hole up.**

Position A#

Using this fingering as interval 1.

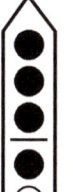

Position 3

< **Start on the 3rd hole up.**

Position 1: Start on lowest hole on the NAF

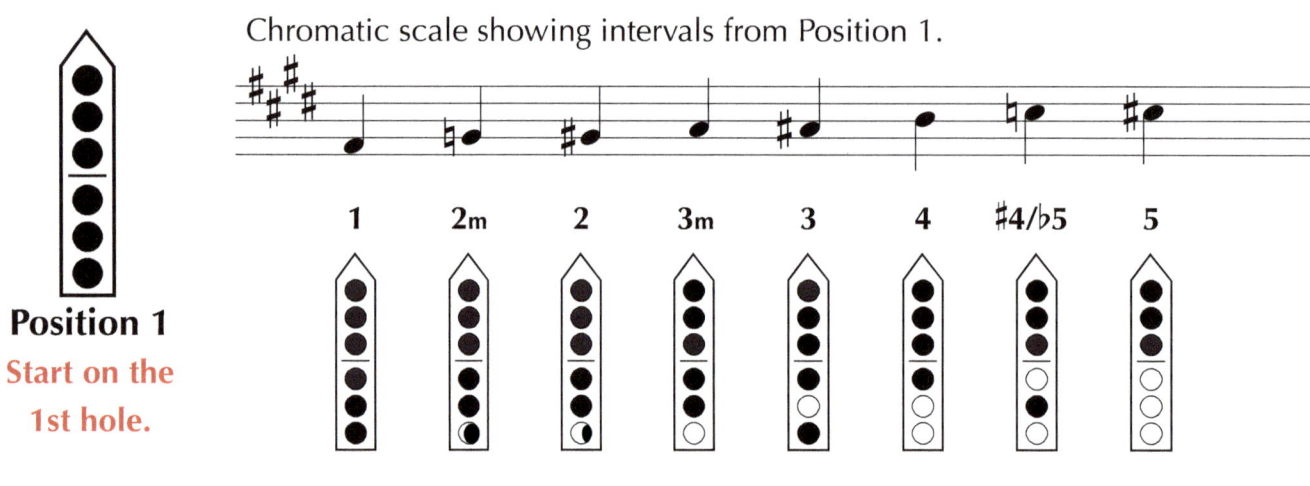

Chromatic scale showing intervals from Position 1.

Position 1
Start on the 1st hole.

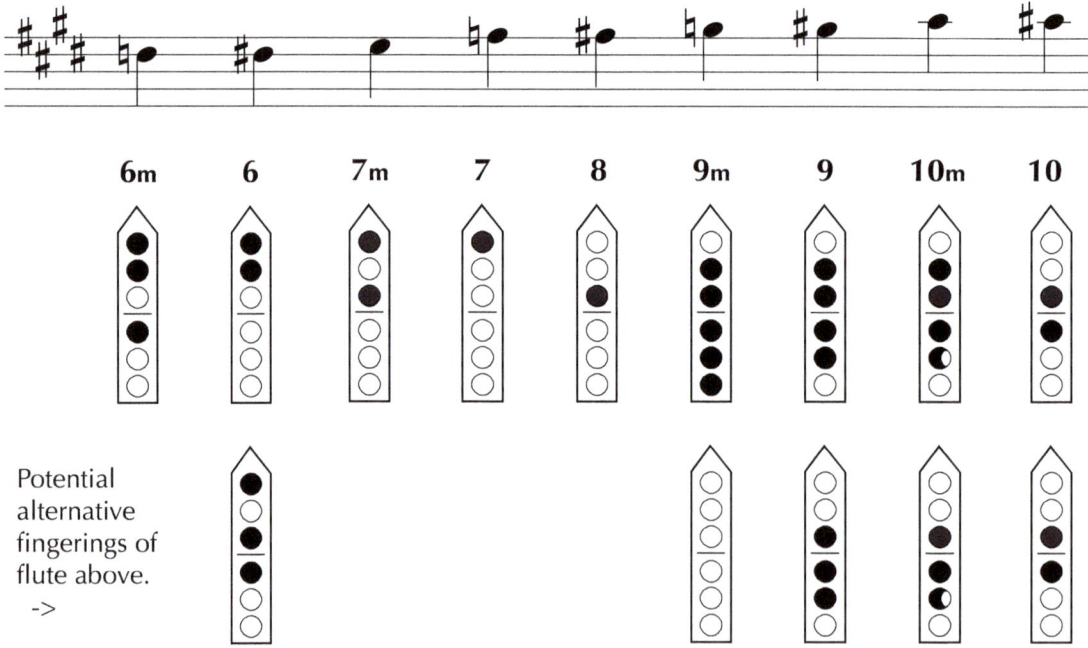

Potential alternative fingerings of flute above. ->

All flutes have their own strengths and secrets. Work with your flute using different fingering positions and breath volume for the best tone. Make sure to give the high notes plenty of breath.

Position 2: Start on the 2nd hole up

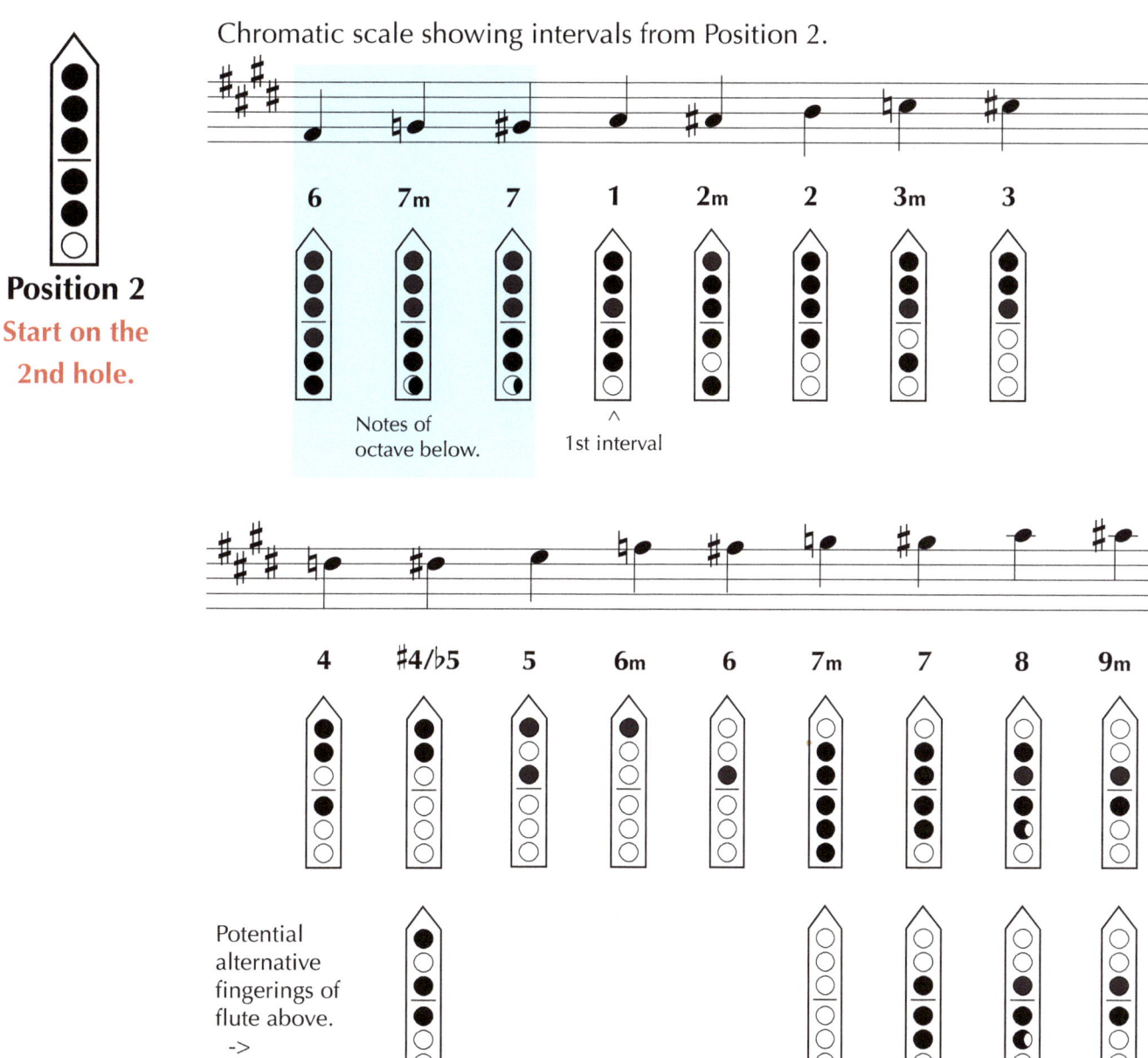

Position A#: : Notice the 1st interval in this position

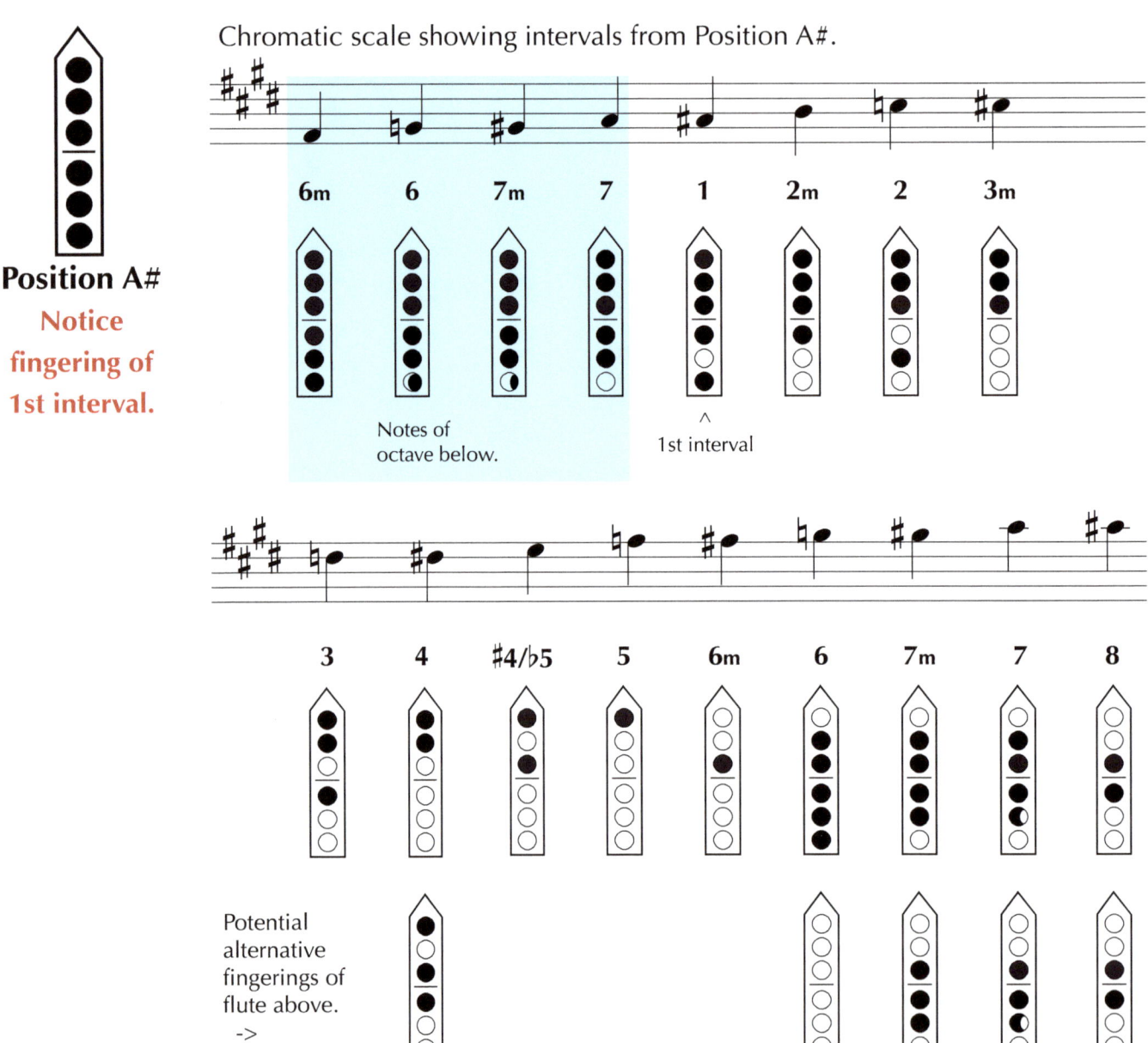

Position 3: Start on the 3rd hole up

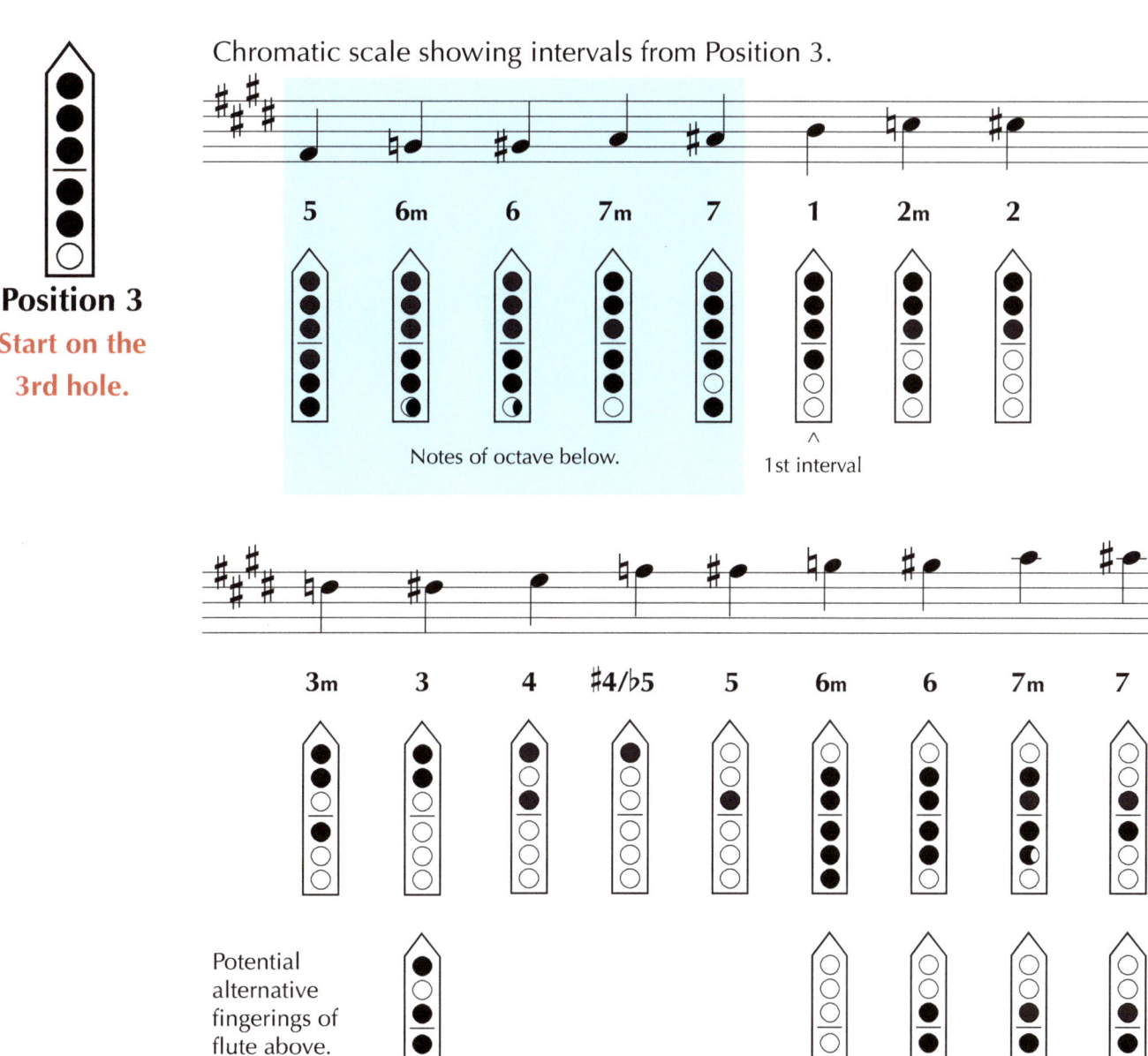

For the Love of Music

Great reviews are the lifeblood of an author's career. Seriously!
If you enjoyed this work, please give it some love by going to your **orders**
on Amazon and letting the world know! Positive reviews really count.

No part of this book was generated by AI. This book was crafted by my hands over hundreds of hours of writing, researching, testing, designing, teaching, and refining.

From my ceremonial musician's heart to yours,

Ami Sarasvati, CMP
Author and Teacher

Loved this book?

There's more to discover! All titles can be found on Amazon as well as:

www.amisarasvati.com

 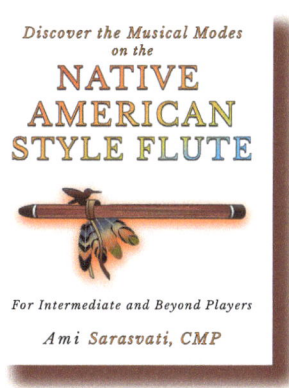 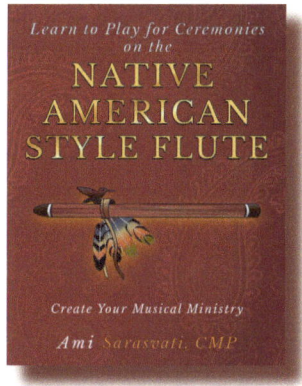 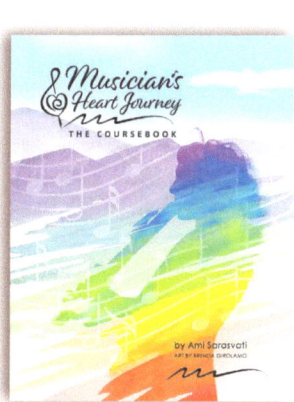